MARJORIE ARCH BURNS

THE TAILORED LOOK

J. B. LIPPINCOTT COMPANY   PHILADELPHIA/NEW YORK/SAN JOSE

Copyright © 1976 by
J. B. LIPPINCOTT COMPANY

All rights reserved. No part of this book may be used or reproduced in any form or by any means, mechanical or electronic, including photocopying, recording or by any information storage and retrieval system, without permission in writing from the publisher.

Printed in the United States of America
ISBN 0-397-40246-5
BICENTENNIAL EDITION

Book design, art, and cover: Ann Atene

This book contains some of the basic principles of the Bishop Method of Clothing Construction from the original texts.

15.7512.1

THE TAILORED LOOK
by Marjorie Arch Burns
Super Sewing Series

TAILORING, EVERYONE?   4

GOING SHOPPING   5
patterns • fabrics • notions

GET READY TO SEW   10
preparing your fabric • trial garment • lay out and cut garment fabric • cutting interfacing • marking

COUTURE TAILORING   22
garment front unit • garment back unit • join front and back units • set-in sleeves • facing unit • collar unit • hem unit lining • lining for garment with cut-on sleeves

SIMPLE TAILORING FOR KNITS AND NON-WOOL FABRICS   57
cutting and applying interfacing • buttonholes • lining

OTHER TAILORING TECHNIQUES   64
shoulder shapes • extra interfacing at shoulders • interfacing curved seam with underlining • piecing fabric and interfacing sleeve heads • topstitching • pleats in sleeves and jacket backs • labels • waistbands • closures • changing points to curves • holding front facings in line • interlining a coat fantastic pockets

PRESSING   110
pressing on grain • moisture • pressure • problems in pressing fabric knowledge • equipment • construction pressing final pressing

TAILORING, EVERYONE?

Want to tailor your own garments but have little time? Think it's too difficult? Simple Tailoring Techniques, beginning page 57, offers time-saving methods for busy people who like to sew. Couture Tailoring, beginning page 22, tells how to tailor wool garments in the traditional way with techniques that are easy to follow.

Tailoring is an art that can be easily learned by reading the instructions for each step through, following them carefully and accurately, and pressing as you go. Fashions and fabrics may change, but basic principles of good construction do not. The techniques given in both sections of THE TAILORED LOOK use these principles. Learn them for a lifetime of tailoring your kind of clothes in fabrics you prefer, to fit you. Use either the Simple or Couture method to tailor fashion garments you will have joy creating and wearing—and that are uniquely yours. Enrich your wardrobe with suits, pants, blazers, coats, and capes. And have fun as you sew. Happy tailoring!

GOING SHOPPING

PATTERNS

If you have never tailored, or if your time is limited, your choice of pattern should be made accordingly. Notched collars, separate front facings (compared to cut-on), set-in sleeves, buttonholes, and use of many fashion details require not only more skill, but more time.

Another consideration is how much wear you expect from the garment. A classic that you will wear for several years deserves more effort in special details.

Blazers, short or long cardigans, wrap jackets and coats, and capes are always in the fashion scene. They can also be made in looks from the sporty to the very dressy by couture or simple tailoring techniques. You may want to study the pattern books and carefully select a pattern that could be used in more than one length in a variety of fashion looks. The very same pattern (for a blazer jacket, for example) can be made in cotton, polyester knit, a blend, wool, evening brocade.

But above all, the pattern must be chosen to compliment your figure.

FABRICS

In recent years there has been a revolution in fabrics that are used for tailoring. Today knits and wovens—even some wools—can be laundered. The important thing when you have chosen the outside fabric is that you also select interfacing and lining that will be compatible—dry cleanable or washable.

There are other considerations. A tailored garment takes more time to make than most other garments and is usually worn longer, so buy the best fabric you can afford. If you have never done much tailoring, select a fabric that is easy to handle for your first tailored garment, so that you can concentrate on learning to tailor, rather than on trying to master a difficult piece of fabric.

At the same time that you carefully select a pattern with lines that are right for you, you must also be sure the pattern is right for the fabric. Suggestions are often given right on the envelope for suitable fabrics — heavy or lightweight, knit, wool, cotton, and so on.

Still another consideration is the difference in technique required for the fabric. Polyester knits, cotton, or cotton-and-dacron fabrics, and some other blends can be tailored much more quickly with the techniques using fusible interfacings shown beginning on page 57.

Wools and most woven fabrics, however, require the couture techniques (pages 22–56). While they require a little more time, the result is a garment of better quality and appearance.

The weight of the fabric is an important consideration. A medium-to heavyweight fabric lends itself to tailoring much better than lightweight fabric. A fabric with a hard finish is more difficult to mold, to press, and in general, to tailor, if you have not had much experience.

Wool is without equal for making a beautifully tailored garment. Wool knits not only tailor more beautifully and make garments of higher quality, they last much longer than polyester knits.

Corduroy and velveteen are popular fabrics, especially for blazers. However, they are not only more difficult to tailor, they do not wear as well as other fabrics.

Another important consideration in choosing a fabric is whether or not it will make a garment that can be dressed up or down. Jackets such as blazers can be very sporty with pants or short skirts. They also can be combined with dressy pants, long dresses, or long skirts for dressy evening wear. Your choice of fabric and trim are important in determining if your garment will lend itself to a variety of fashion looks.

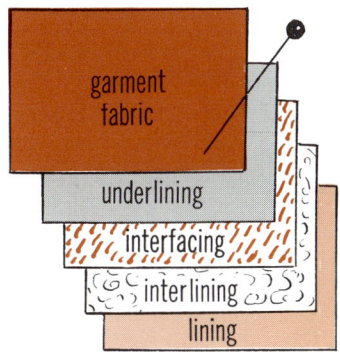

Be aware of what the best designers use in tailored garments. Besides the fabrics already indicated—wool and wool knit—designers tailor raw silks, heavy cottons, linens, even brocades. Often upholstery and drapery departments offer a variety of these fabrics in good weights and at favorable prices.

Finally, but of greatest importance, is suitability of the fabric for you. The right color can add magic. The scale of design and the texture are important considerations, too.

INTERFACING

Interfacing is used for shaping and support in the body of the garment—at neckline, fronts, shoulders, armhole edges, and hems.

There are just as many decisions to be made about your choice of interfacings as there are in your choice of outside fabric. They must be compatible to the outer fabric—dry cleanable or washable. They can make or break the finished garment. At the same time that they must have enough weight to support the outside fabric, they must never impose themselves on the outer fabric—be stiff or boardlike. The best way to determine this until you become a real pro is to lay the two over your hand and see how they work together.

Non-woven interfacings come in various weights just as the wovens do. Very frequently two weights of interfacings are used in one garment for desired effects in different parts. Woven interfacings with some wool content shape and mold easily. Those with goat hair content do not crease easily and have to be handled differently at facing edges, as shown on page 16.

When muslin or lightweight woven fabric is required in this book make certain it is preshrunk as well as grain-perfect. Interfacing for the back of a garment is usually cut from a lightweight fabric such as unbleached muslin or a cotton-and-dacron broadcloth in matching color if the interfacing shows through garment fabric.

The nonwoven interfacings are usually used in knits. Polyester is the most popular type; it comes in many weights. Some nonwoven interfacings are called bias, which means they have more give. (Actually, nonwoven fabrics have no grain direction.)

Nonwoven interfacing may or may not be fusible. Use of fusibles in tailoring is described beginning on page 57. Specific directions for applying fusibles accompany each brand.

UNDERLINING

Underlining gives support to the entire garment. It is also used to give body to a fabric that is too weak or lightweight or is too loosely woven to tailor. Underlining is lighter in weight than interfacing, and it also serves as a layer to conceal interfacing in a loosely woven or light-colored fabric. It should be chosen to match or enhance the color of the outer fabric. Instructions for underlining are on pages 68–70. It is important that underlining also be compatible with the outer fabric—drycleanable or washable.

LINING

A garment is interfaced or underlined for character, shape, and body, but it is lined mainly for appearance—to give a couture finish. A lining eliminates finishing seams, facings, and hems; it makes the garment easier to put on and take off; it feels luxurious.

The lining must be compatible with the fashion fabric in weight and texture, and it should conceal the inner construction. As a rule, it is softer and lighter in weight than the outer fabric. It should not be stiff; it should conform to the garment and should not distort the way it hangs. Lining finish should be smooth and slippery in order to put on and take off the garment easily. The lining should conform to care requirements of fashion fabric—both should be drycleanable or both should be washable.

Lining can add personality to a tailored garment. It can be a colorful contrast to your outside fabric. It can match a scarf, blouse, shirt, dress, or skirt. You may select a print, dot, stripe, or plaid. If you have a great scarf that you no longer wear, it could be outstanding as the lining for the front of a jacket. Use a plain lining for the back and sleeves. Select a matching lining, however, if your garment will be worn open over a variety of colors or designs in blouses, dresses, or sweaters. If your lining is of an expensive fabric, select something less expensive for the sleeves.

Some popular lining choices are twill, crepe, satin, silk, or a silk look in a fiber that is compatible with your fabric and that you can afford. Do not skimp on the quality of the lining, however. Buy the best you possibly can. An elegant lining emphasizes the look of quality in a beautifully tailored garment.

NOTIONS

The notions you will need are those that are used for a professional pressing job. These are shown on pages 112–113. Of course, you also will need zipper, buttons, and snaps as indicated on your pattern envelope.

GET READY TO SEW

PREPARING YOUR FABRIC

Always preshrink fabric. Fold wool in wet cloths or sheets for 2–3 hours. Permit to dry. Launder washable fabrics. Remember:

1. Long naps (cashmere, mohair), wool broadcloth, and other napped fabrics should not be processed in the manner indicated for wools. Instead, hand-block with moisture and heat. Any other technique may mat the nap and cause creasing. (See page 120 for blocking technique.)
2. Fabrics that may crease from folding in wet cloths should be kept flat, covered with wet cloths, then plastic, and allowed to remain until moisture penetrates.
3. If you feel the center fold will be a problem to press out, shrink wool flat.
4. Fold fabric in accordion folds if necessary to store.
5. Press woven interfacings and linings to straighten the grain.

TRIAL GARMENT

A great deal of money usually goes into a tailored garment. It is an important part of a wardrobe and will be worn for a long time. For these reasons it is an excellent idea to test your pattern in a trial garment for size, appearance, and fit. A trial garment can be made from and old sheet or inexpensive fabric. On the other hand, a trial garment made from denim, seersucker or corduroy can become an inexpensive jacket, coat, or robe. This trial garment is the place to check jacket length in proportion to the skirt or pants that will be worn with it, the proportion of the lapels, size and placement of pockets, the set and size of the collar, the number and placement of the buttons. Blazers and cardigan jackets are so useful in wardrobes that you may reuse a pattern often.

Testing your pattern also eliminates excessive handling of the garment fabric. If you will not wear the trial garment, trim off hem allowances from the sleeves and bottom of garment, as well as seam allowances from outside edges of collar, pockets, lapels, and so on. Then the trial garment will have the same proportions as your finished garment.

The button and buttonhole at the bustline should be on a direct line with the crown of the bust. If the position of these must be changed, all of the buttons and buttonholes will need to be respaced. If this results in raising the top buttonhole, the shape of the lapel may also need to be raised to accomodate this change. The lapel shape should be redrawn before cutting your fashion fabric, and this change also should be made in the lapel facing and interfacing.

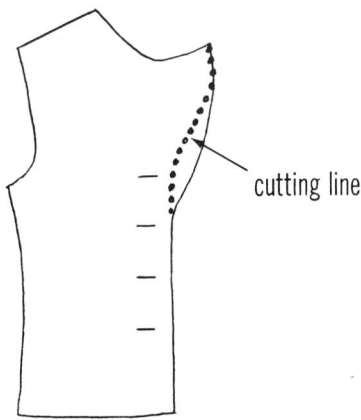
cutting line

LAY OUT AND CUT GARMENT FABRIC

NAPPED FABRIC

A pattern layout for a napped fabric includes pile fabrics as well. Because of the effect of light on the surfaces of nap, the color and texture of a napped fabric can appear to vary according to the direction of the nap. To avoid this kind of variation in a garment, all garment pieces should be cut with the tops the same direction of the nap. This is the reason it is so important to follow the layout for napped fabric if you are using one.

Woven pile fabrics should be cut with the nap direction up on the garment pieces. Corduroy, suede cloth, velveteen, and velvet are woven pile fabrics. All fabrics with nap (brushed surfaces) should be cut with the nap going down, as should fleece, camels' hair, and any of the fake-furs and deep-piled fabrics. They not only will look better, but they will wear better if cut this way.

If you are not sure of the direction of the nap, run your hand gently over the fabric. The direction in which the fabric feels smooth and rather silky is the direction of the nap. The direction in which the fabric feels rough is against the nap.

Mark the top of the fabric. Napped fabrics should be folded with wrong sides together so the fabric will not slip during cutting.

ONE-WAY DESIGNS

Some fabric textures show definite designs. Examine yours closely. If it does, all the garment pieces should be cut with the tops in the same direction. Other fabrics may have printed designs with a definite top and bottom. These are not always large prints, so check your fabric carefully. Use layouts for fabrics with nap for all these. Other fabric surfaces that may reflect light differently according to the direction of the cut are satins, moirés, and iridescent silks. When sewing such fabrics inspect them carefully in the light to determine the direction you want the pieces to be cut, be sure to cut them all in the same direction.

Some polyester double knits and woven fabrics have a very slight nap or design that is not always easily detectible but will reflect light differently. They should be cut one-way.

CHECKS, PLAIDS, AND STRIPES

Checks, plaids, and stripes require special layouts, in many cases, in order to match designs at seamlines where garment pieces are joined. A number of attractive effects can be obtained in this way, but such matching requires experience and skill. It is not recommended that beginners attempt it.

In general, if the distance from one complete design to another is one-fourth inch (6mm) or less, it is not necessary to match the designs at the seamlines. However, if you are using such a fabric, avoid any pattern with seamlines on the straight of the grain, because it may join two light or two dark lines in a seam.

Cut checks, plaids, and stripes in a single layer. After cutting the first piece, use it as the pattern for laying out and cutting the second. The second piece is cut exactly like the first so that the designs will match perfectly.

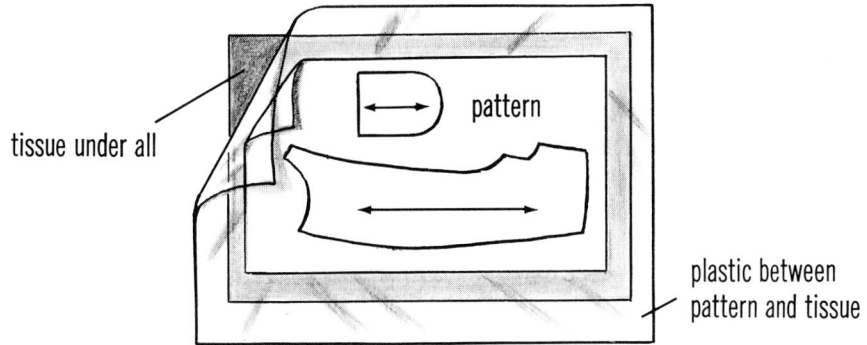

HEAVY FABRICS

Reinforce the pattern with plastic to prevent tearing from repeated use. Lay a plain tissue paper on your pressing board. Place over it a thin sheet of plastic (an opened cleaner's bag). Cover with a second tissue. Press slowly with a warm iron until the two layers of tissue are bonded to the plastic. Trim off excess paper and plastic, but not the pattern margin. If you do not wish to reinforce the pattern, be sure to cut interfacing before cutting fabric. (Pinning the pattern to heavy fabric can tear it.)

EXTRA NOTCHES

Extra notches are very helpful for matching garment pieces precisely. Use them at the following points:

1. Top of the sleevecap where it joins the shoulder seam.
2. Underarm of two-piece sleeve where it joins garment side seam.
3. Front or back of bodice at center fold where it joins skirt, collar, or facing.
4. Front or back of skirt at center fold where it joins bodice or waistband.
5. Collars, facings, yokes, and waistbands at center folds where they join other garment pieces.

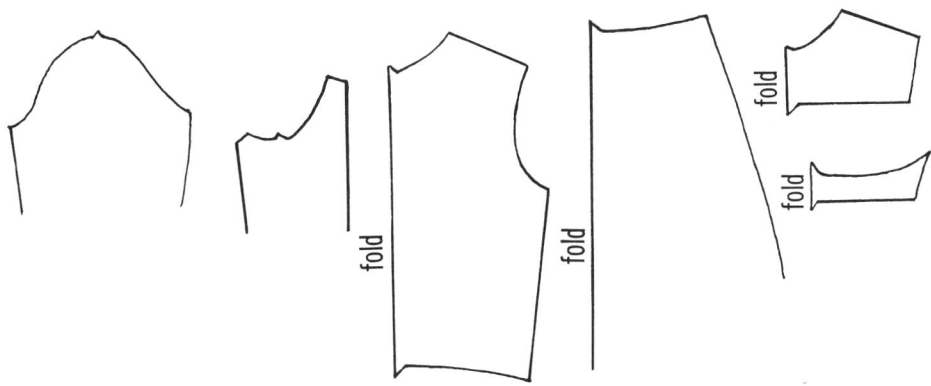

COLLAR

Read about the tailored collar (pages 32–37) before cutting it; or place pattern on fabric as directed, but do not cut collar until you are at that point in construction. Depending upon weight of fabric, it may need to be cut a little larger.

The interfacing for the collar is cut from the same interfacing that is used in the front of the garment. This will give the same character to both parts of the collar-lapel unit. Cut interfacing exactly like the under collar. If the commercial pattern gives a separate tissue for cutting the interfacing all-in-one on the bias, eliminate this piece and cut from under-collar pattern (two pieces) for best results.

If the commercial pattern does not show true bias for the under collar and interfacing, redraft grain line as shown, and cut both on true bias. All this is important to do so that the collar will mold easily, roll softly, and lie uniformly at the neckline.

If you are tailoring a bulky fabric, the undercollar can be cut of a lightweight fabric—knit or flannel. These fabrics also make excellent facings, and the contrast in texture and/or color can add interest to the garment.

It may be desirable to cut the top collar on a bias fold instead of the straight fold the pattern gives. This would be done only if the fabric is very firm and will not mold easily to the neckline. It is not possible to do this with plaids, checks, or similar designs; the bias

fabric	fabric wrong side
underlining	
interfacing either side	interfacing either side
interlining either side	
lining	lining wrong side

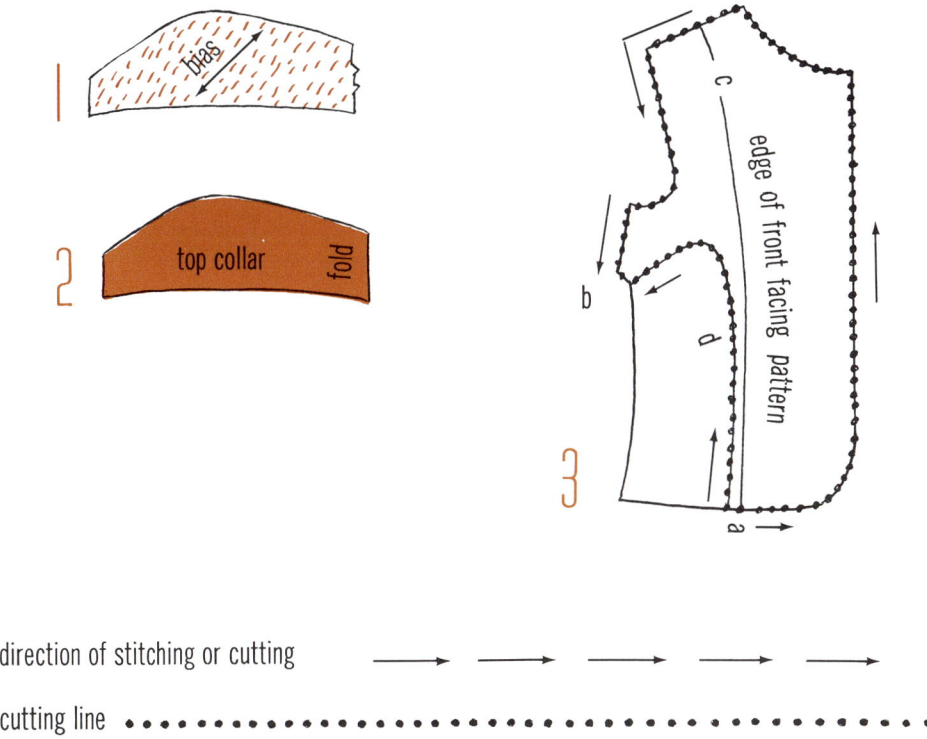

direction of stitching or cutting →→→→→

cutting line • • • • • • • • • • • • • • • • •

line at the front ends of the collar would give an unbalanced design. Check your layout before cutting collar.

CUTTING INTERFACING
Unless the pattern company has given separate pattern pieces like those in the following directions for cutting interfacing, use the original pattern pieces to cut the interfacing. Be certain interfacing is on true grain before beginning to cut. It is cut on same grain as the garment.

INTERFACING FOR SEPARATE FRONT FACING
The interfacing for a separate front facing is cut exactly like the pattern for the front of the garment from point **a** to **b** [approximately 2 inches (5cm) below the armhole]. With tracing paper and wheel mark center front, buttonholes, and any darts.

To complete cutting interfacing, key pattern for front facing in place on top of interfacing. Cut along line **d** ¼ inch (6mm) beyond edge of front facing up to bustline; then swing out and cut freehand to meet point **b**, as shown. If the front pattern is in two or more pieces, cut interfacing in the preceding manner, but in separate pieces like the garment.

INTERFACING WITH MUSLIN STRIP, FOR SEPARATE FACING
If the interfacing you are using is wiry and will not press to give sharp, thin front edges (goat hair, for example), it should be eliminated from the facing seamline. To do so, cut a strip of muslin to extend from center front to lower edge of garment 1¼ inches (3.2cm) deep. Cut on identical grain of interfacing and from the same pattern piece.

Place muslin strip on wrong side of interfacing. Match outer edges of strip and interfacing. Stitch ⅞ inch (2.2cm) from edge; stitch again at inside edge of muslin for reinforcement. Press to smooth the stitching line.

Trim away interfacing to first row of stitching ⅞ inch (2.2cm) from edge. Staystitch to garment when ready.

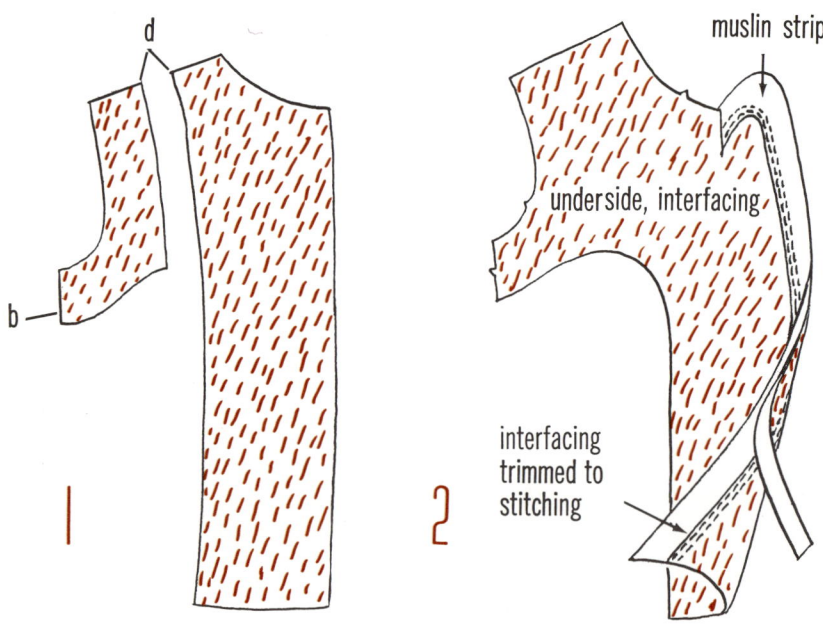

FOLDBACK FACING
If your pattern has a foldback facing, see pages 66–68.

BACK INTERFACING
Interfacing for the back of the garment is cut from a lightweight fabric such as unbleached muslin. A dacron-and-cotton broadcloth, matched to the garment color, may be used if white would show through.

Cut the back interfacing as shown. Use the garment back pattern from **a**, 3 to 5 inches (7.5 to 12.5cm) down the center back, around to **b**, 2 inches (5cm) below the armhole. Mark back shoulder darts with tracing paper and wheel. Remove pattern and cut freehand from **a** to **b**. If the back of the garment is cut on the straight of grain, the seam may be eliminated in the interfacing and the center back placed on the fold when interfacing is cut.

If the back pattern is in several pieces, cut interfacing on the same grain as garment, using the same principle, but cut in separate pieces as the garment is cut.

BIAS STRIPS FOR HEM AND SLEEVES
True bias from mediumweight interfacing, 1½ inches (3.8cm) wider than hem width, is needed to cushion the hems of garment and sleeves and to give body to these lower edges. Cut enough for these areas. When sewing strips together overlap ¼ inch (6mm) on true grain, and stitch at machine.

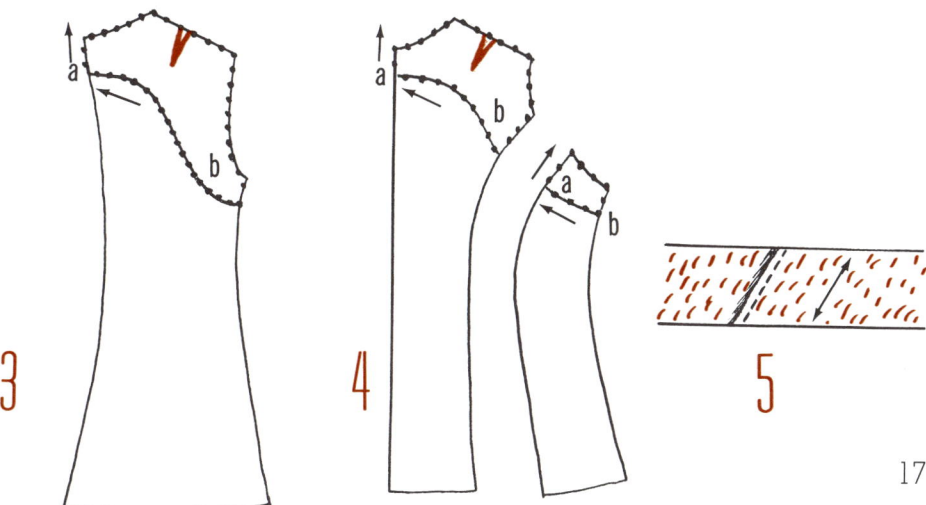

Place interfacings in units with their respective garment pieces. Cut lining after garment has been fitted (instructions, pages 66–68).

MARKING

It is extremely important to mark accurately, because each mark indicates where some construction detail is placed. The only construction mark on the pattern that will not ordinarily be transferred to the fabric is the seamline, but beginners should mark those if they are curved or appear in any way to be difficult to stitch. Otherwise the seamline can be accurately determined by using your machine guide.

There are several methods of transferring markings to your fabric. Except for tracing threads, markings are transferred to the wrong side of the fabric.

TRACING PAPER AND WHEEL

This is the method that is easiest. It can be used on most fabrics to transfer line markings. Some heavyweight fabrics, however, will need to be marked one layer at a time, and some fabrics may not take the carbon marks. You should try the carbon first on a small scrap of your fabric.

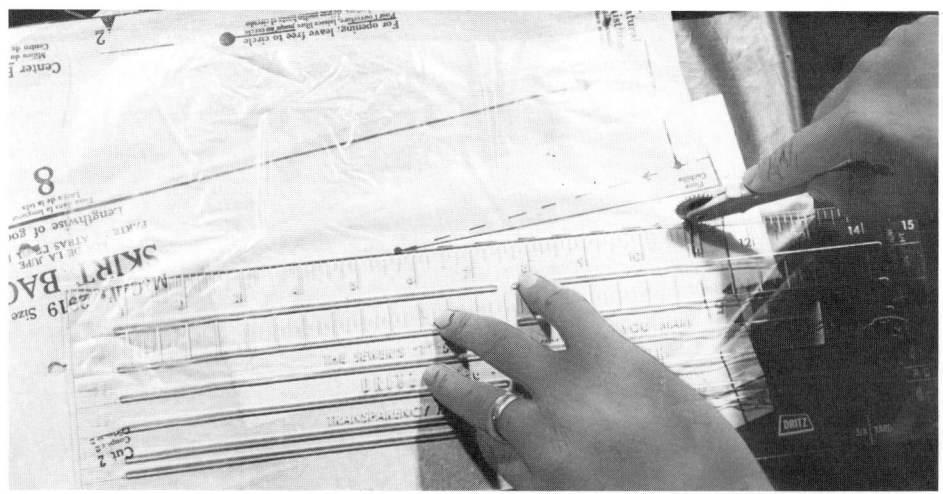

Marks from your tracing paper should be removable by laundering or drycleaning. Use the color of tracing paper closest to the color of your fabric that still will be visible.

Tracing paper can be used economically by cutting it into strips just wide enough for the marks you will be transferring—the width of a dart, for example.

To mark two thicknesses of fabric with right sides on the inside and pattern tissue on top, fold the coated sides of tracing paper together. Slip the top half of the tracing paper between the pattern tissue and the fabric and the bottom half under the lower garment piece. Both carbon sides should be against the wrong sides of the fabric. Roll the tracing wheel away from you over the marking lines. For straight lines use a straight edge such as your ruler to guide the wheel. Mark each line only once; do not retrace. On curved lines, mark slowly; use your fingers or a French curve, if you have one, to guide the wheel.

To mark darts, remove just enough pins from the pattern to slip the tracing paper under the tissue. Trace a line down the exact center of the dart. (This is the pickup line, on which the dart will be folded.) Then trace the outside lines. Mark the termination point (the point where the dart ends) with a small crosswise line.

For fabrics that are hard to mark, reinforce the marking lines of the tissue with cellophane tape or cover with a sheet of thin plastic to prevent the wheel from tearing the tissue. After tracing check to see if the marks have been transferred to the lower fabric layer. If they have not, remove the tissue and top layer of tracing paper, leaving the bottom layer of tracing paper in place. Trace with the wheel over the marking on the upper garment piece.

THREAD TRACING
Thread tracing is a way of transferring markings to the right side of your garment. These might be placement lines for pockets, lines for pleats, center front and center back garment lines. The last enable you to check the hang of your garment after construction. Mark each garment piece separately with a long basting stitch or a running stitch, taking a small backstitch at the beginning.

CHALK AND PINS

Another technique for marking darts and other lines is to place pins with small heads on stitching lines through tissue and fabric layers. With tissue in place, turn over both layers of fabric. Lay your ruler along the stitching line indicated by the pins, and mark the stitching line with chalk. Turn pattern side up. Remove pattern without shifting pins.

Mark this side in the same way before removing pins.

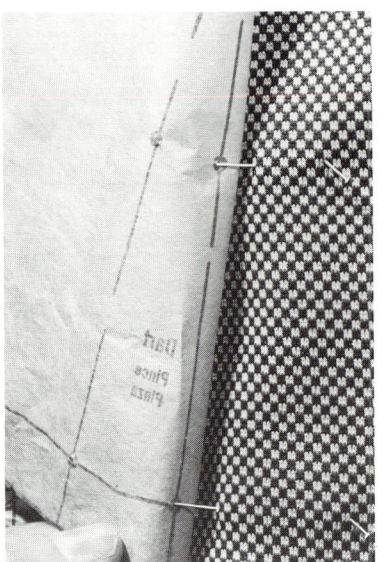
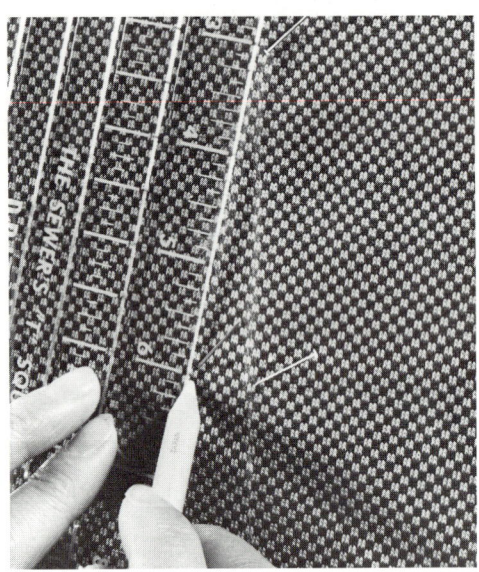

TAILOR'S TACKS

Tailor's tacks can be made in different colors of thread for each type of marking—darts, circles, squares. They are useful because they can be seen on both sides of a garment piece and because, when different colors are used, the different markings can be distinguished easily. Although they may be more time-consuming,

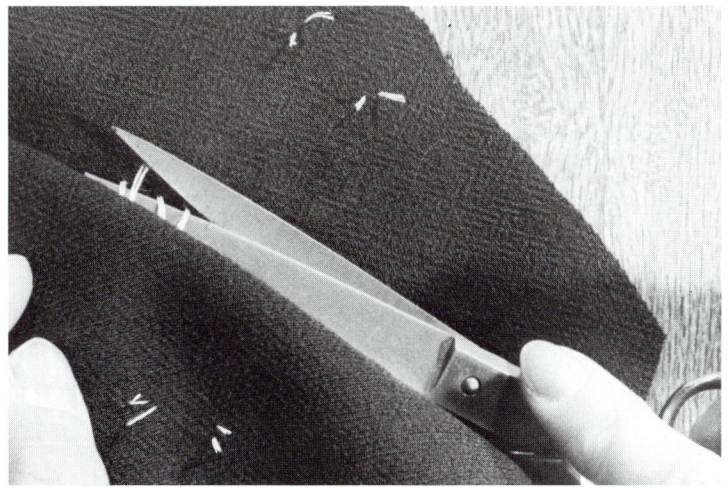

they will be worth the time for a pattern with a complex design that has a number of kinds and sizes of markings.

Tailor's tacks can be done through both layers of fabric and the pattern. Use an unknotted double thread. (Have needles threaded with as many different colors as you have types of markings to transfer.) Take a small stitch through the center of the marking as shown; make sure you have caught both layers of fabric. The end of the thread should extend from the stitch about 1 inch (2.5cm). Take another stitch through the same spot, leaving a loop large enough for your finger to fit in. Clip the thread but not the loop, leaving about an inch (2.5cm) of thread on the clipped end. If there are a series of marks in a line as for darts or pleats, stitch the entire line, making sure there will be enough thread for a 1-inch (2.5-cm) end on each side of each tailor's tack.

When all of the marks on the pattern have been tacked, lift the pattern gently off the fabric without pulling on the stitches. Carefully separate the two layers of fabric, clipping the loops to leave tufts of thread on both layers. If you need to mark a straight line, you can then do so (on the wrong side) by aligning a ruler along the tacks and drawing between them with chalk.

COUTURE TAILORING

How to tailor a woven fabric — wool, silk, linen, for example — into a beautiful suit, coat, or jacket will be shown in this section. Wool knit can be tailored this way, too. However, if you want to quickly tailor a wool or polyester knit or one of several cottons or blends, techniques for doing so are given beginning on page 57.

The method for tailoring a garment with a traditional notched collar, set-in sleeves, and lining are shown here. Instructions for details — buttonholes, pockets, and so on — begin on page 64.

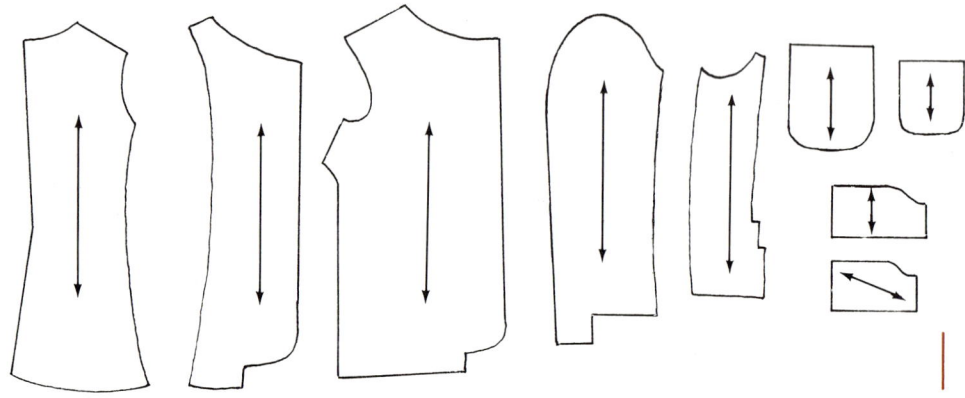

GARMENT FRONT UNIT

DARTS IN GARMENT

2. Permanently stitch darts unless they need to be basted for fitting. Trim dart to a ⅜-inch (1-cm) seam as far down as it is that wide. At end of slash cut into dart at an angle halfway to stitching line.

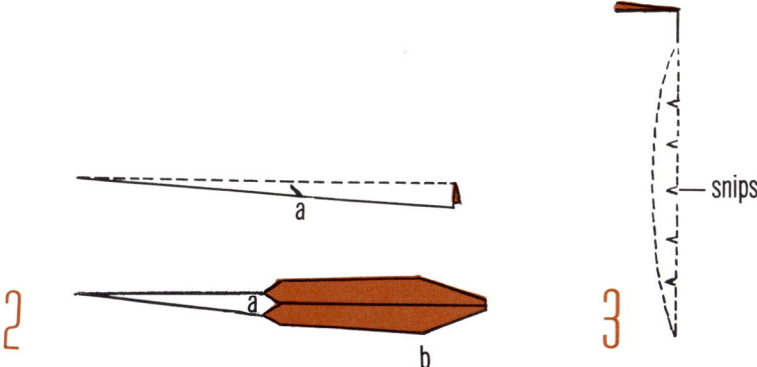

Press seam open. Below opened seam use a metal knitting needle to separate dart as you press. Press on each side of stitching line all the way to the point. Beginning 1¼ inches (3.2cm) from raw edge, trim seam away diagonally at **b** to ⅛ inch (3mm) to eliminate bulk at seamline.

Waistline darts are snipped to help them lie smoothly. They are pressed toward the center front or back. Press bust darts down.

DARTS IN INTERFACING
Slash one side of dart marking all the way to point **a**. Lap slashed edge to second dart line. Stitch close to edge; then stitch ¼ inch (6mm) back from edge or use wide zigzag stitch for reinforcement. Trim away excess interfacing in dart to second stitching line. For reinforcement, zigzag with machine stitch at point of dart.

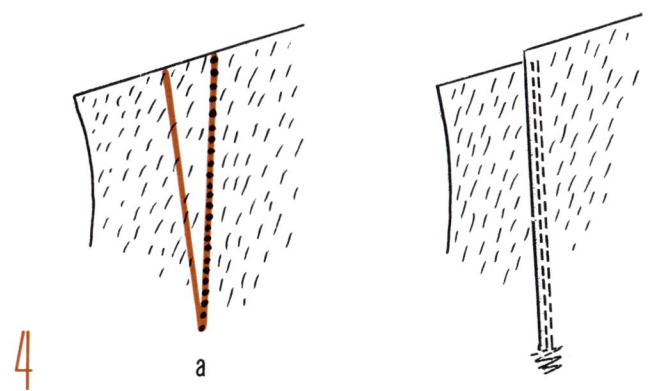

STAYSTITCHING FRONT UNIT

Place interfacing on underside of garment front. Key to perfection, and press if necessary. Pin in place, keeping pins back from the stitching line.

At the corner of the lapel, the interfacing is cut away ¼ inch (6mm) beyond the seamline. Do this wherever there is a corner in the garment — collar, pockets, and so on — to reduce unnecessary bulk.

Although sometimes you will be sewing against the grainline, usually it is easier to staystitch the interfacing to garment fabric all around with interfacing side up. Interfacing will not push out of line under the presser foot as the softer garment fabric might do.

All staystitching is done at ½ inch (1.3cm) except edges **a** and **b**, which are done on the seamline. Because the collar and facing will be attached here the interfacing can be trimmed away more easily later.

Baste the crosswise lines and the center front for buttonhole locations from interfacing through to outside of garment. Always baste crosswise lines before lengthwise ones. On fragile fabrics — those that would be marked by machine stitches, such as velveteen — use hand basting. See page 30 to attach facings now.

If you have tested your garment pattern, it will be easier to make buttonholes in the garment front now instead of having to handle the entire garment when it has been sewn together. See buttonholes, page 86. Your pattern may show pockets, or you may decide on style, number, placement yourself. Excellent techniques for various pockets are given from page 94. If you have tested your pattern, it is easier to make pockets now, also.

GARMENT BACK UNIT

PREPARE INTERFACING

Stitch the center back seam of muslin interfacing unless seams have been eliminated by cutting the interfacing on the fold. Press seam **a** open and trim to ¼ inch (6mm). Slash one line of dart marking all the way to the point **b**. Lap slashed edge to second dart line. For reinforcement stitch once close to edge and again ¼ inch (6mm) from 1st row, or use a wide zigzag stitch. Trim excess muslin in dart to second stitching line. Repeat for second dart.

STITCH GARMENT BACK/APPLY INTERFACING

Stitch center back seam on seamline in correct direction, and press open. Beginning 1¼ inches (3.2cm) from neck edge, trim seam diagonally to ⅛ inch (3mm) to eliminate bulk at seamline **a**. If garment may require fitting at this seam, then stitch permanently only as far down as muslin interfacing will extend (marked with arrow, **y**) and press. Machine baste the remainder of seam until garment is fitted. Baste waistline darts, if any, until garment is fitted.

Stitch back shoulder darts permanently. Slash for a depth of 1¼ inches (3.2cm) at fold of dart, and finish like the dart on page 23.

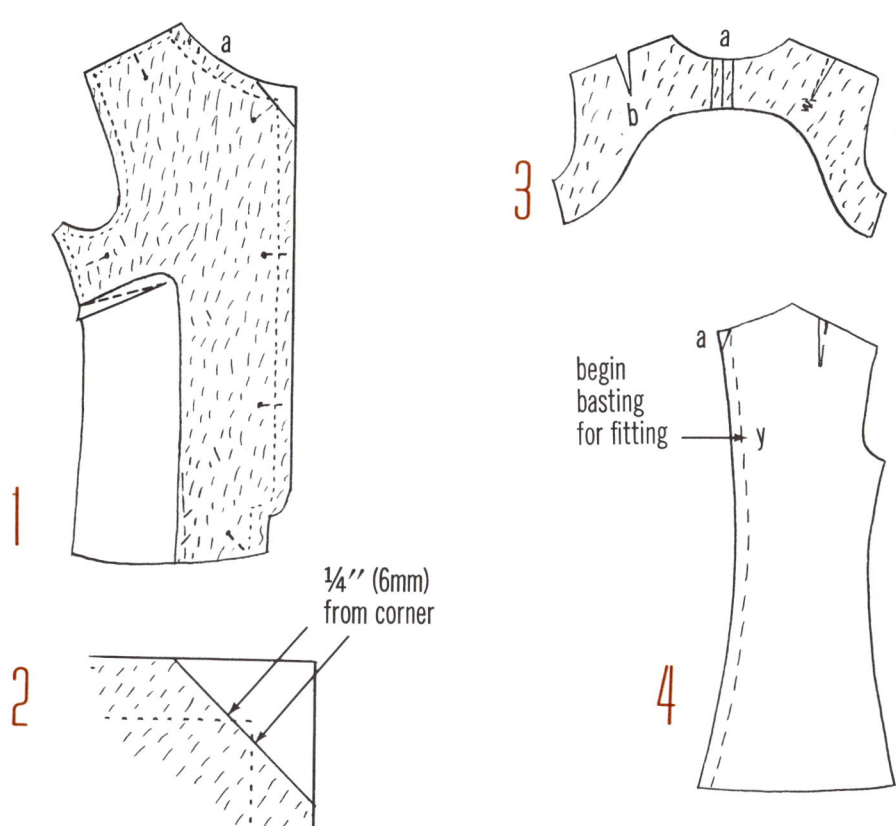

Place finished side of interfacing next to underside of back. Staystitch interfacing to back just outside seamline as shown.

JOIN FRONT AND BACK UNITS

Stitch shoulder and side seams in correct grain directions (page 26). When stitching one shoulder seam, the back of the jacket will be on top; in stitching the second, the front will be on top. This does not matter. The correct direction for stitching is of importance. If garment may require fitting at these seams, baste them until fitting is completed. Then the seams are stitched permanently and basting removed. Trim seams diagonally at points **b** and **c** as at **a**, center back. Do not trim interfacing from shoulder seams; it remains the width of seam allowance for reinforcement at shoulders. If you have much fitting, it may be wise to cut and sew the lining (pages 44–50) immediately after you have fitted the garment, while the alterations are fresh in your mind. Then proceed to the rest of the garment construction.

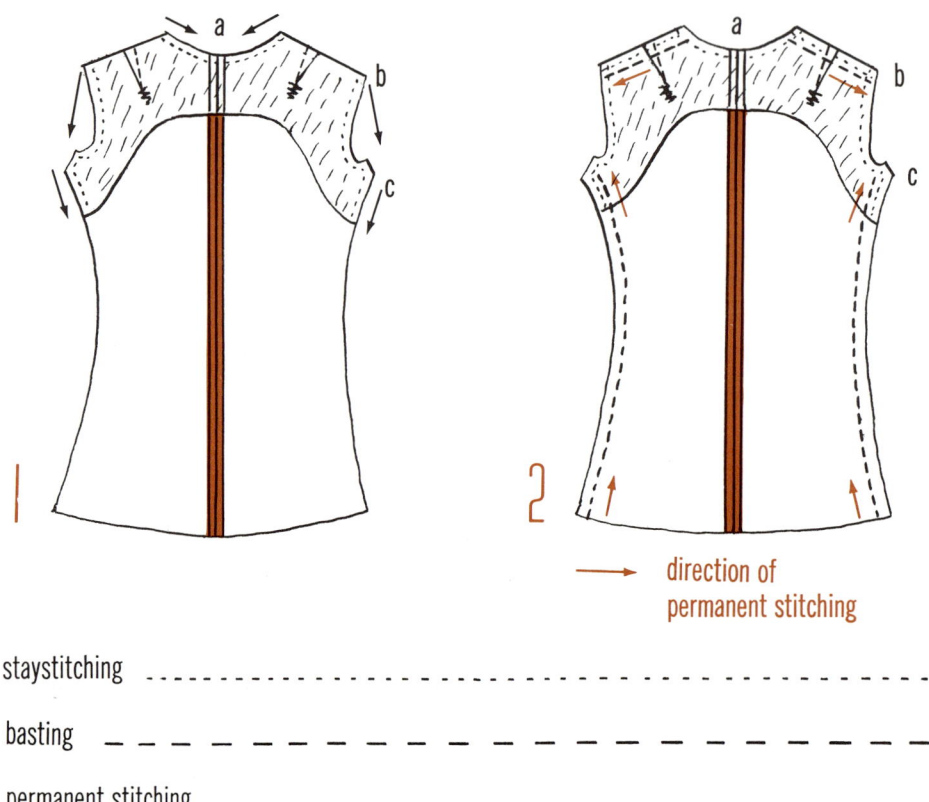

direction of permanent stitching

staystitching ....
basting   — — — — — —
permanent stitching _____

SET-IN SLEEVES

OFF-GRAIN STITCHING

If it is a two-piece sleeve, with right sides together join upper sleeve to under sleeve at back, sewing from top down. Press seam open in same direction in which it was stitched, and trim diagonally at upper edge for 1¼ inches (3.2cm).

This advanced method for setting in sleeves is called off-grain stitching. When preparing the cap to fit in the armhole, stitch it while the fabric is held off-grain. The sleevecap is easier to manage before the outside sleeve seam is stitched. Use matching thread to stitch around entire cap ½ inch (1.3cm) from edge with a regulation stitch. Below the notches use staystitching; above the notches use off-grain stitching.

To do off-grain stitching, place forefingers opposite each other in front of the needle. Pull fabric off grain, and stitch four to five stitches where fabric is pulled. Stop the machine before lifting the fingers to pull next area. When fingers are placed in front of the needle, start the machine again. Both hands must be kept on the sleeve cap; they cannot be used to operate the machine. Certain fabrics, because of a firm weave or finish, will need to be pulled more than others before stitching. Once the rhythm of off-grain stitching is developed, caps can be made to fit the armhole with perfection. If the cap does not fit the armhole with this method in the first trial, remove the stitching and try again. It will not harm the cap.

The sleevecap requires most ease where it is most off-grain, above the notches, in the middle third on each half of the cap.

FINISH SLEEVES

If you have already tested your pattern, then you can finish the lower edge of the sleeve while it is still open, which is much easier. If you are not certain of the length, baste the second sleeve seam and baste sleeve in armhole for fitting. Remove basting after fitting, and complete sleeve as follows:

Turn up hem to correct finished length and press on grain from folded edge to hem edge. A sleeve should not carry a hem deeper than 1½ to 2 inches (3.8 to 5cm). Trim width of seam allowances in hem at **b** to ¼ inch (6mm). Trim a little beyond fold of hem.

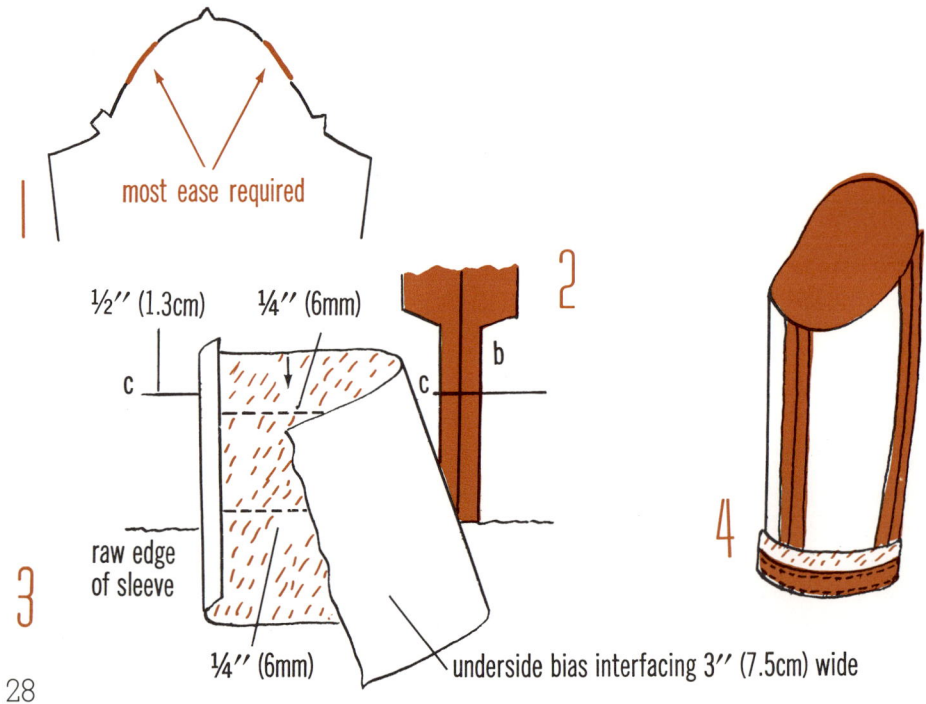

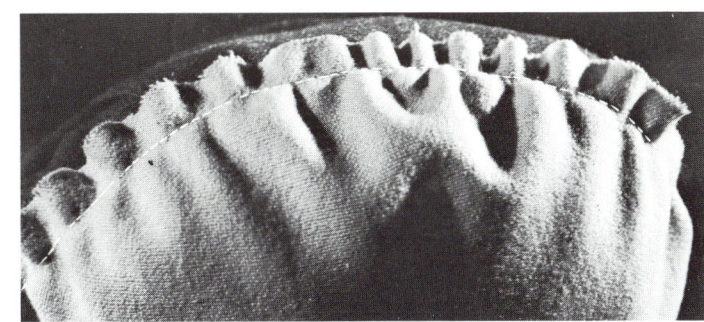

6

5

A 3-inch (7.5cm) wide bias strip of interfacing (page 42) is used to cushion the edge of the hem. Place it to extend ½ inch (1.3cm) beyond the fold of the hem **c**. With sleeve side up, stitch bias to hem ¼ inch (6mm) from raw edge of sleeve and ¼ inch (6mm) from fold of hem. Bias extends above hem to cushion it. Press hem again, and block bias to bottom of sleeve with perfection. Blocking is discussed on page 120.

Open out hem, and stitch second sleeve seam from armhole down. This front sleeve seam needs to be held firmly on the lengthwise grain as it is stitched; it even may need to be clipped in some fabrics. Press seam open in same direction in which it was stitched. Restore hemline at seamline. Trim this seam to ¼ inch (6mm); trim a little beyond fold of hem. Do not tack hem in place until directed. Block bottom of sleeve from right side. Use loose basting to hold up hem until sleeve hem is completed. Shrink out ease of sleevecap on end of cushion. Steam press with point of iron at seamline to form a smooth, round cap.

You may prefer to wait to insert sleeves in garment until the sleeves have been lined (page 49) and the collar, facings, and hem units are completed.

Basting in one sleeve is usually enough for a fitting. It is then removed to complete all steps of sleeve construction. This eliminates handling the entire garment and is more professional and easier to do.

INSERT SLEEVES IN GARMENT
Pin sleeve in armhole with two pins, one pin matching underarm notch on sleeve to underarm seam on garment, the other matching extra notch at top of sleeve to shoulder seam. The sleeve should always be on top and garment beneath for stitching. Begin stitching somewhere under the arm, and continue all the way around the circle, sewing one thread inside off-grain stitching.

The armhole seam is not pressed at all from one notch to the other at underarm. Lay cap and garment together on the cushion with sleeve on top. Press with point of iron at seamline. When completed, seam will turn into and lie in sleeve, but it is not pressed into sleeve. This gives the armhole a rounded, rolled look at the cap of the sleeve. Do not trim any of the seam allowance or any interfacing from armhole until ready to stitch in lining (page 50). If your sleeve cap needs any reinforcement, see page 73.

FACING UNIT
It was suggested earlier that if you had already tested your pattern, it would be much easier to make the buttonholes and pockets in the front before sewing the garment together because there is much less to handle. This is also true for attaching the facings, but you can decide.

Staystitch edges **a** and **b** exactly on the seamline. These stitches on the seamline serve as important keys for stitching on the collar and sewing in the lining. Also staystitch back facing at **c** and **d** exactly on seamline. If your garment has a foldback facing, refer to pages 66–68. In bulky fabrics, you can eliminate the back neck facing and cut the lining like garment back to meet collar at neck-

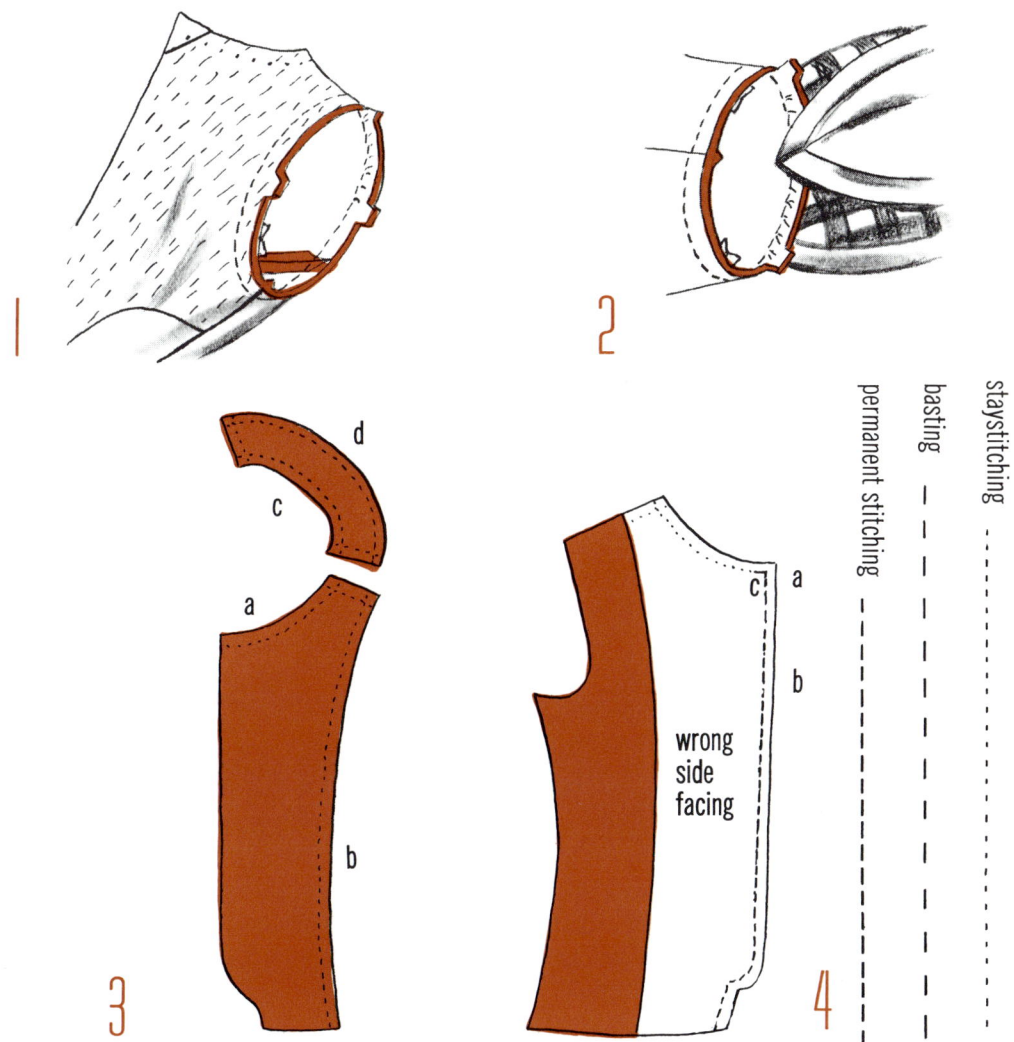

line. Place facings on garment fronts, right sides together. Ease facing to garment above top buttonhole (between **a** and **b**). This will prevent the facing from having a tight drawn look when it turns back over garment to form the lapel. Facing will be held firmly to garment below top buttonhole. Sew facing to garment with garment side up through staystitching on seamline. Use short reinforcement stitches at **c** on lapel for 1 inch (2.5cm) for greater strength in corner. Do not sew facing to garment beyond corner of lapel yet.

First press seam open; then grade it. Trim interfacing close to the seamline. This is easy because you have made the staystitching on seamlines in areas that must be trimmed.

From top of lapel to top buttonhole trim the garment seam allowance, **a**, to ⅛ inch (3mm) and the facing, **b**, to ¼ inch (6mm). Below the top buttonhole, trim just the reverse—facing, **c**, to ⅛ inch (3mm) and garment, **d**, to ¼ inch (6mm). Repeat for other half of garment in same relation to top button placement. The wider seam serves as a cushion for the narrower seam below, preventing its showing on right side of garment when pressed.

Next, turn facing and press it. Always press the underside first to set this edge; then turn to garment front to final press. Make certain all edges of the garment and facing meet with perfection at **a**, **b**, and **c**. It is easy to distort them in pressing.

After edges have been set in place with the iron, the pounding block is used on the outside of the garment to obtain sharp, thin edges without iron shine on wool and other heavy fabrics. Steam an area just the length of the block, quickly remove iron and pressing cloth, and slap garment with the block. Hold block firmly for a minute or two. This forces out the steam and leaves flat, sharp edges. Repeat if necessary. See photo, page 122.

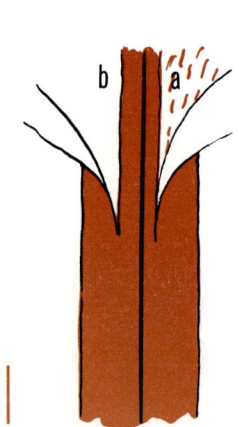
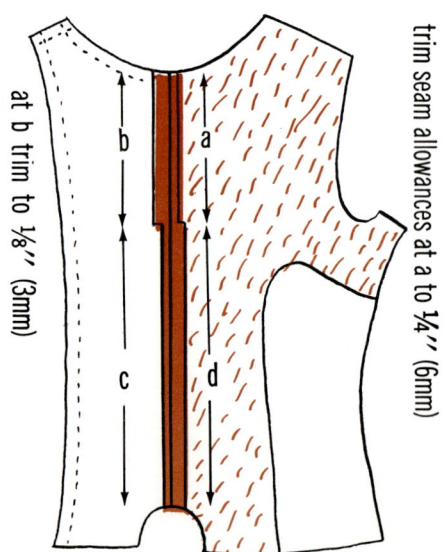

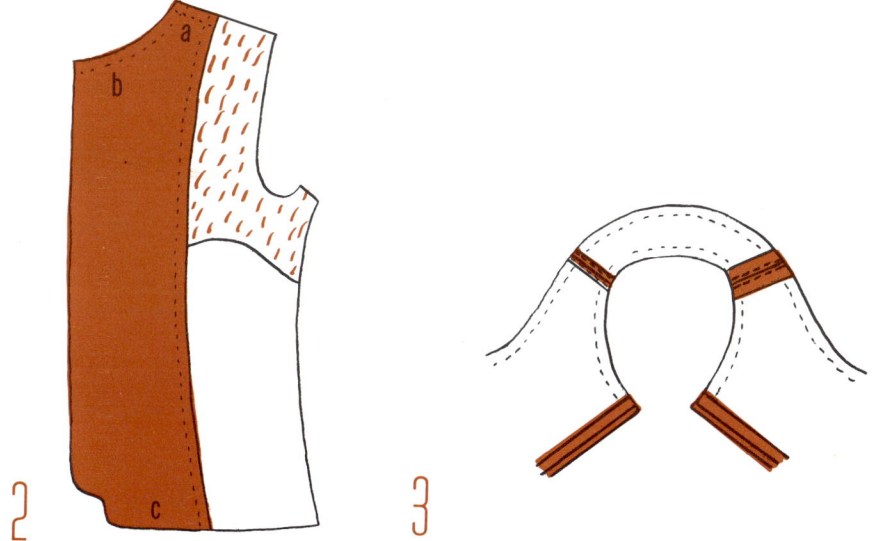

At shoulders, join back facing to front facings on seamline. Press seams open; topstitch each side of seams, and trim away seam allowances to topstitching. This technique can be used any time you want to eliminate bulk at seamlines in a facing of heavy fabric.

COLLAR UNIT

With a large collar or one from heavy or bulky fabric, the top collar may need to be cut ⅛ to ¼ inch (3 to 6mm) deeper at edges **a** and **b**, tapering to nothing at **c**, to allow for turn-of-the-cloth. (When you roll a magazine, the outside seems smaller than the inside; this is the principle of the turn-of-the-cloth.)

The only way to determine if the top collar will be large enough is to make the under collar with the steps that follow, and baste a trial top collar to it. Roll the two over your fingers to see if the top collar is large enough.

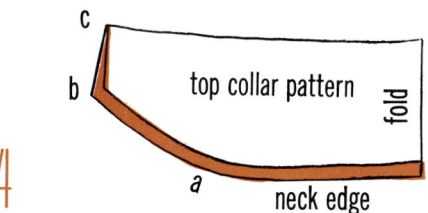

If you learn this after the collar is cut out, cut a small amount from the under collar and interfacing at **a** and **b**, tapering to original line at **c**; or use less than a ⅝-inch (1.5-cm) seam allowance on top collar when sewing the two together.

Place two sections of interfacing together for the under collar. Use two pins at **a** and **b** to hold bias interfacing in place. Using dressmaker's tracing paper and wheel, mark a stitching pattern for the under collar.

The stitching pattern can form various designs, providing lines are on crosswise and lengthwise threads of interfacing. At the outside corners cut interfacing diagonally beyond the seamline to eliminate bulk. Staystitch interfacing to under collar between ½ and ⅝ inch (1.3 and 1.5cm) at neck edge, and ¾ inch (5cm) from outside edges **b** and **c**.

Stitch center back seam of under collar and interfacing. Press open. Trim away interfacing to stitching line at center back seam. Topstitch each side of the seam beginning at neck edge and continuing down one side to ¾ inch (2cm) from outside edge, **c**. Cross over to other side, and topstitch up to neck edge. At roll line of collar, while topstitching use staystitch plus: Press index finger firmly against back of presser foot so fabric piles up against finger and threads of fabric are crowded together. Release and repeat until the roll-line area has been stitched. This helps the collar to roll into place. Trim away all of garment seam allowance except last ¾ inch (2cm) that is not topstitched (at **c**).

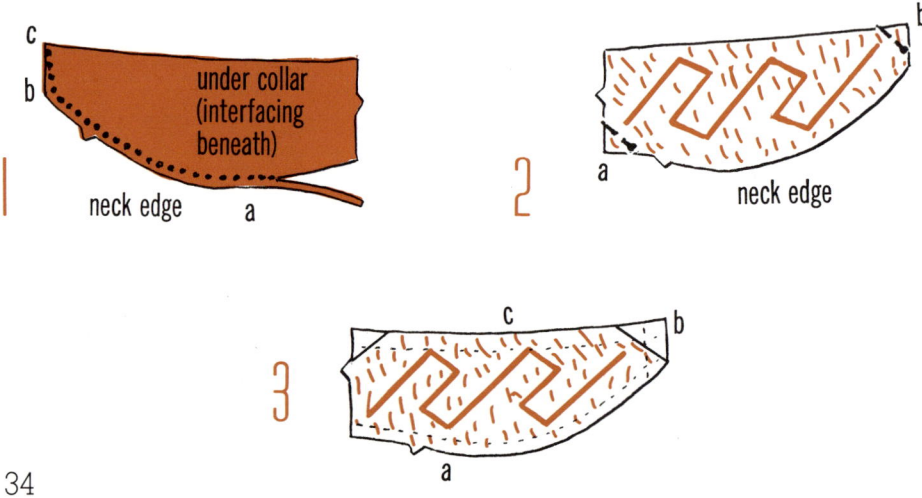

34

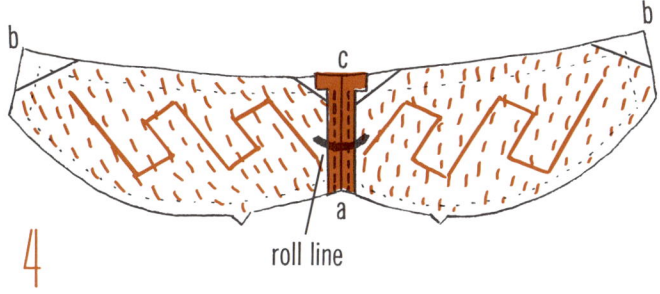

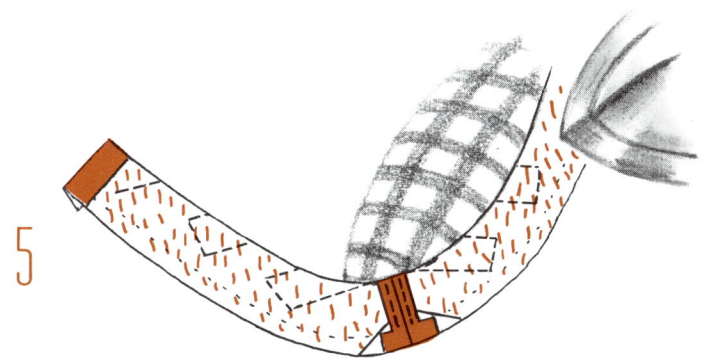

With interfacing side turned up, quilt entire under collar at machine on lines marked for stitching. Stitching must always be on grain when crossing from one line to another. It must not extend beyond the staystitching around collar edge. With fine fabrics, the quilting may be done by hand with a small running stitch.

Mold the under collar on a cushion to curve it at the neckline for a close fit. Fold it in half lengthwise with interfacing side out, and pin to hold. Fold seam allowances of ends back toward collar, and pin to hold. Mold half of the collar on the cushion at a time. Place steam iron down on edge of collar to hold collar on cushion. With left hand, curve collar while pressing on grain up to fold of collar. Continue to curve collar with left hand and press with iron in right hand until the under collar takes on a curved shape. The aim is not to stretch the outside edge of the collar, but to press in a breaking point for the collar at the neckline. Repeat for the other half of the collar. Remove pins to give a final shaping. Allow collar to cool and dry completely on the cushion after shaping before continuing with construction.

A large collar is treated differently. It will not break at the center back. Instead of folding it in half at the center back, fold only about a third of the collar back at the neckline to form the curve. Press the seam allowance back at the outer edges of the neckline. With this exception, press as in preceding paragraph.

Trim interfacing close to ¾-inch (2-cm) staystitching line at outside edges, and trim garment fabric to point at center back seams.

At this point in construction, try on collar. Pin-baste seamline of under collar to seamline of jacket and check how collar sets when worn. It may look and feel more comfortable if it is lowered at center back—it can be lowered as much as ¾ inch (2cm). To do this the collar will need to be a little larger for the larger circle, so take less than ⅝-inch (1.5-cm) seam allowance at the ends.

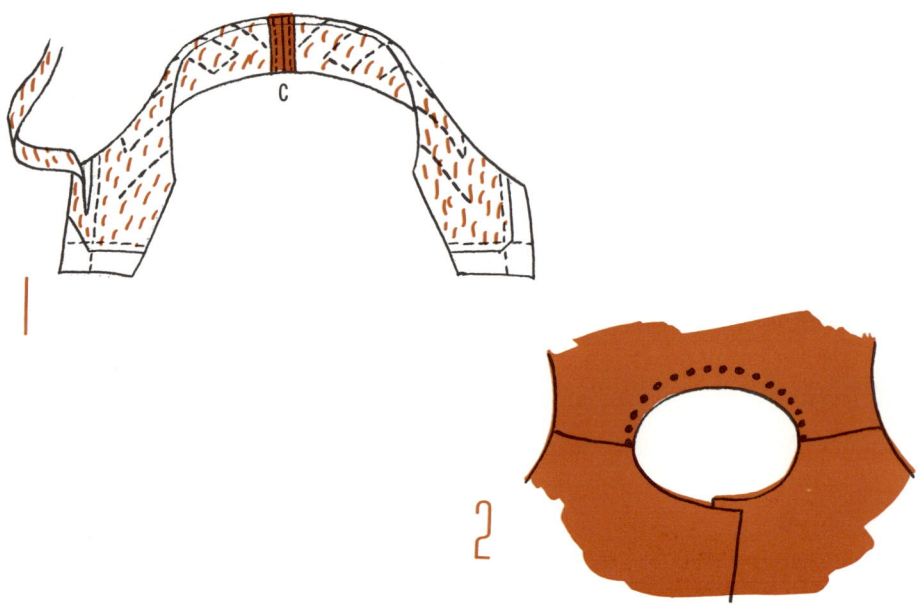

At outside edge **c** stitch top collar to under collar, right sides together. If collar is rounded stitch them together around curve, but leave open at least 1 inch (2.5cm) at neck edges. Begin and end with 1 inch (2.5cm) of short machine stitches. Match center back of top collar to center back of under collar perfectly. Keep collar side on top, and stitch on the seamline so the interfacing is not stitched. The staystitching will show on the underside of the completed collar.

Press seam open, and stagger edges of seam allowances. The upper collar seam allowance is trimmed to ¼ inch (6mm) and the under collar seam allowance to ⅛ inch (3mm). Bevel the edges when cutting heavy fabrics (hold the scissors at a slight angle to fabric as you cut). This makes the cut edges bias and less blunt so that they will not mark the outside fabric during pressing. In tailoring all faced edges of seam allowances are staggered, or graded. (This also is true of heavy fabrics in dressmaking.)

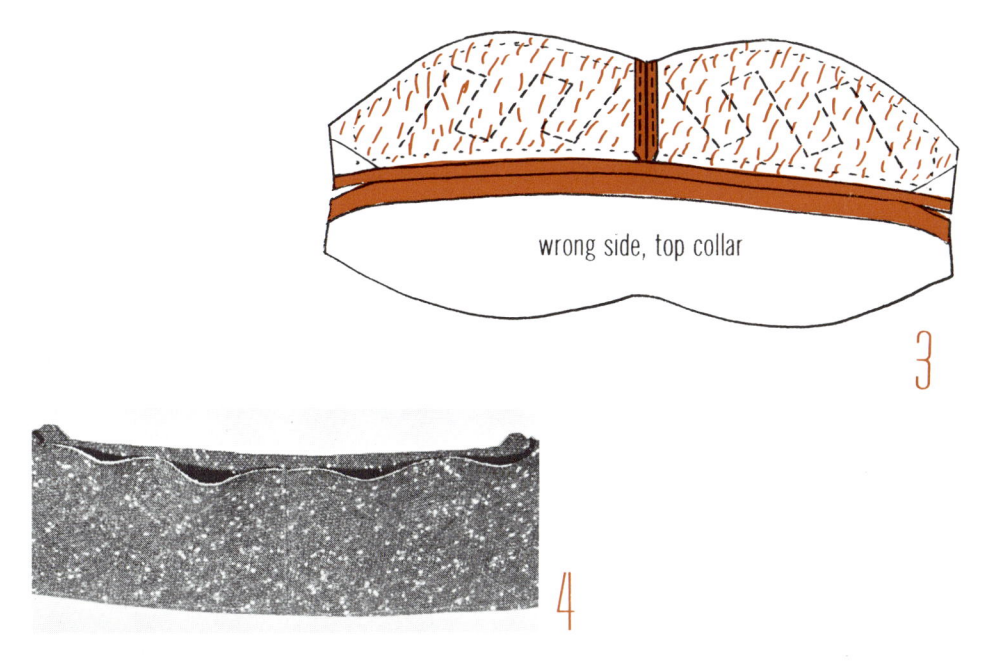

Whenever the under collar and interfacing are bias, the collar is not understitched because the bias controls the edge of the under collar.

Turn collar right side out. To set the outside edge, keep under collar on top, and press along stitching line. Turn over (top side up) to press and pound. Top collar will appear to be wider than under collar until it is stitched to garment.

37

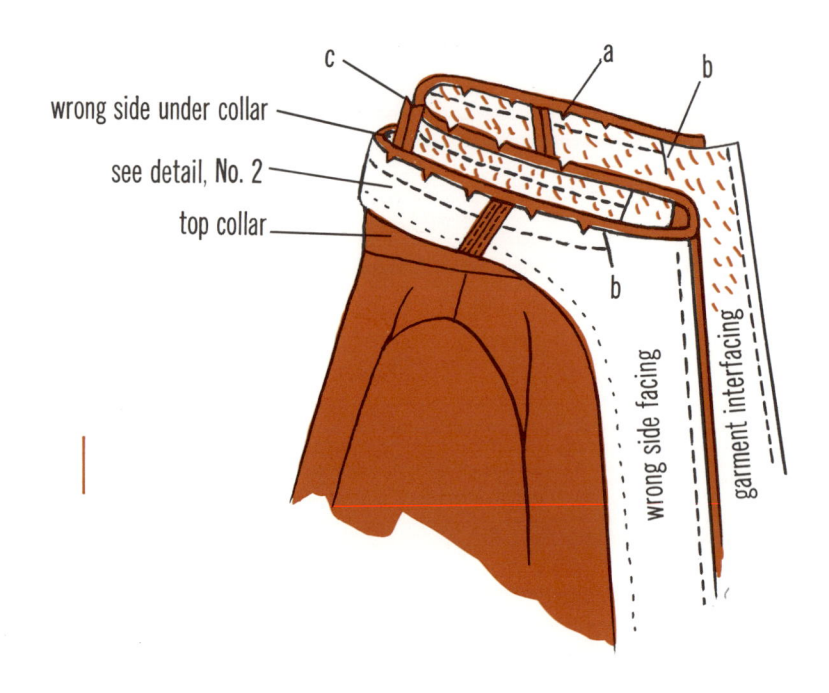

1. At intervals clip neck edge, **a**, of garment almost to staystitching to give a straight line for stitching. Make certain that markings on garment and front facings indicate location, **b**, of finished ends of collar. Key and pin center back of under collar to center back, **c**, of garment neckline. Key and pin seamline of ends of under collar to neckline location marking, **b**. There is a shoulderline marking on collar to key with shoulder seam. (This is important, so that ease will be distributed evenly.) Ends of collar are still open. With garment side up, stitch under collar to garment on seamline from one location marking to the other.

2. Clip neck edge, **a**, of facings at intervals almost to staystitching to give a straight line for stitching. Key and pin center back of top collar to center back, **c**, of facing. Key and pin seamlines of each end of top collar to location markings, **b**. Key the shoulderline markings on collar with shoulder seams. With facing side up, stitch top collar to facings on seamline from one location marking to the other.

38

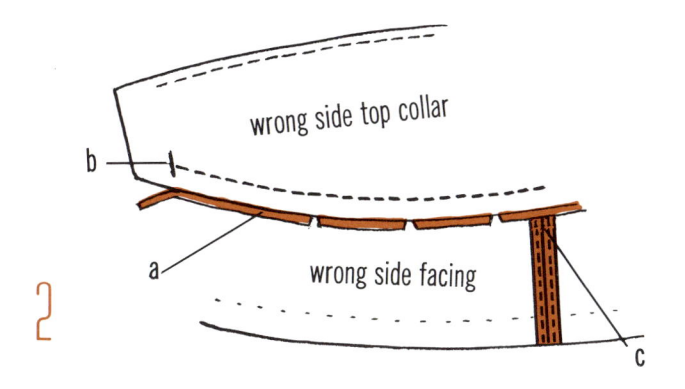

With right sides still together, close ends, **a**, of garment lapels. Stitch from outer edge to location markings, **c**, at neckline, which have been keyed with pins.

Next, close ends of collar, **b**, to location markings, **c**, already keyed with a pin. This is not a continuous operation; ends must be closed separately. During these steps, turn all neckline seams away from stitching line. Trim corners as shown.

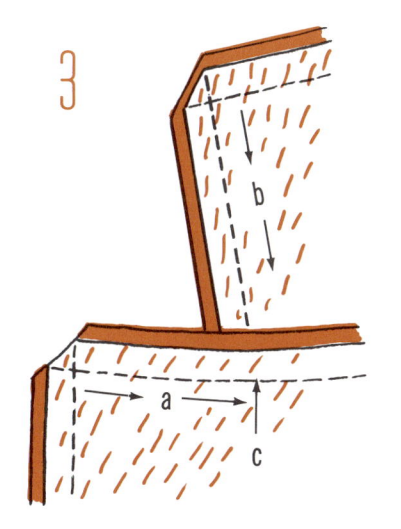

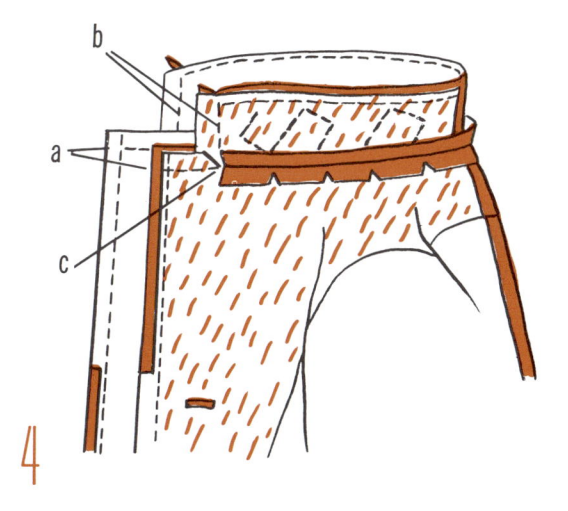

To attach this collar a four-point closure was used — four seams stitched separately but all meeting at one point, **c**. This is a technique you can use many places.

Using edge presser press seams open, and stagger seam allowances to ¼ inch (6mm) on top and ⅛ inch (3mm) on underside, as described previously.

Next, using edge presser press top collar, **a**, and under collar, **b**, seams open. To complete the collar, trim interfacing to seamline, and grade the top collar seam allowance, **c**, to ⅜ inch (1cm), the under collar seam allowance, **d**, to ¼ inch (6mm). These are the seam allowances that turn upward inside the collar. Turn collar right side out.

Sew the remaining untrimmed garment-facing seam allowances with a single thread, **e**. Use a loose running stitch, close to the seamline. Then grade these remaining untrimmed seam allowances: top collar ⅜ inch (1cm), under collar ¼ inch (6mm).

Final press collar and front facings. Using a press cushion, shape and mold the collar and front facing into a single, well-tailored lapel unit. They will not be treated as separate collar and facing units again. Use iron directionally on fabric grain. You may even hang garment on a hanger, or place it on a form, if you have one. Holding steam iron a few inches away, steam lapel area again. Mold with hands, and dry completely.

Whether your coat or jacket has a separate or a cut-on facing, it is always easier to leave the ends of the collar and lapel open until the collar has been sewn to garment.

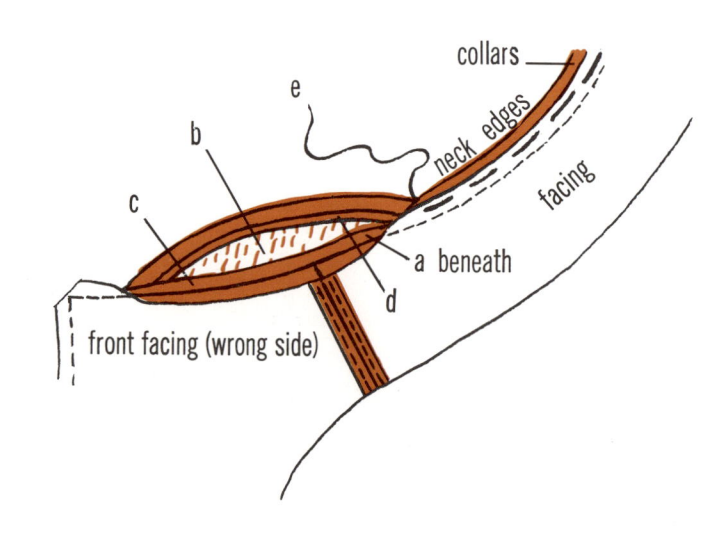

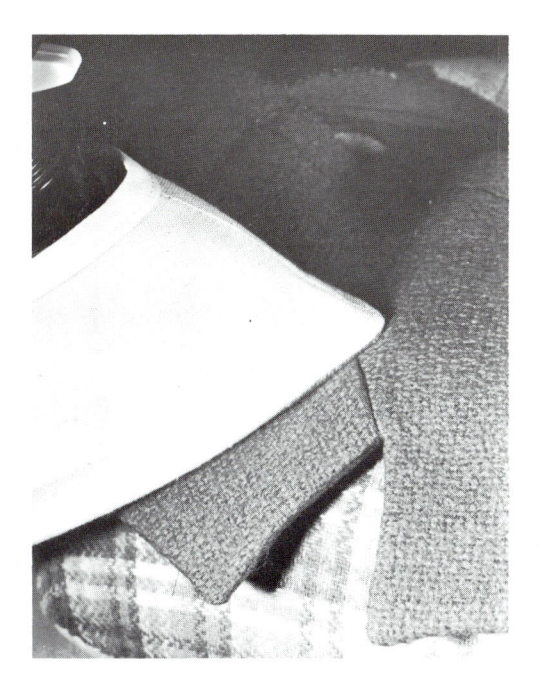

HEM UNIT

In tailoring, it is helpful to think of the facing, collar, and hem units as one complete circle of construction steps; all are vital to turning out a quality, couture garment.

Press up hem desired amount. A jacket usually has 1½-inch (3.8-cm) hem, a coat, 1½- to 2½-inch (3.8 to 6.3-cm). At hemline, trim vertical seam allowances to half their width to a little beyond depth of hem. Use staystitching plus or easing ¼ inch (6mm) from edge of hem. Press hem again directionally from fold to top of hem; upper edge should match garment perfectly, and all seams should be keyed to match.

← hem foldline

Cut bias interfacing to be placed inside the hem, 1½ inches (3.8cm) wider than the hem. Fold up ½ inch (1.3cm) on one long edge, and press lightly; do not stretch bias while pressing. You may stitch the bias ½ inch (1.3cm) from edge to act as a bridge for turning, if necessary. The ½ inch (1.3cm) will turn up in fold, toward the hem. Block the bias into hem, and pin at intervals; there can be no suggestion of fullness on bias; nor can it be tight. Ends of bias should overlap on front interfacing about ½ inch (1.3cm). Loosely stitch bias in place, first at fold of hem, catching only one thread of the garment to bias at ½-inch (1.3-cm) intervals. Do this from right side of garment. Next, at staystitch plus line, loosely stitch bias to hem only, with stitches ½ inch (1.3cm) on underside, and an invisible, small stitch on the top.

Press hem up again, block to perfection, and pin at intervals. The hem is not stitched to garment until lining is inserted (see page 51). You may want to run a loose basting stitch ¼ inch (6mm) up from fold to hold hem in place until lining is completed.

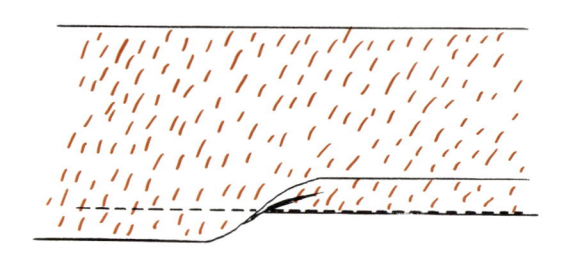

fabric	fabric wrong side
underlining	
interfacing either side	interfacing either side
interlining either side	
lining	lining wrong side

42

To make a good sharp bend or fold where the facing and garment join at the hem, trim both sides of facing seam allowances to a scant ⅛ inch (3mm) to top of hem. Pin well of garment hem seamline to well of garment front seamline, and stitch (hand or machine) from right side of garment in well of the seams to top of hem. Stitching will not show, and it enables facing to roll back easily and press flat.

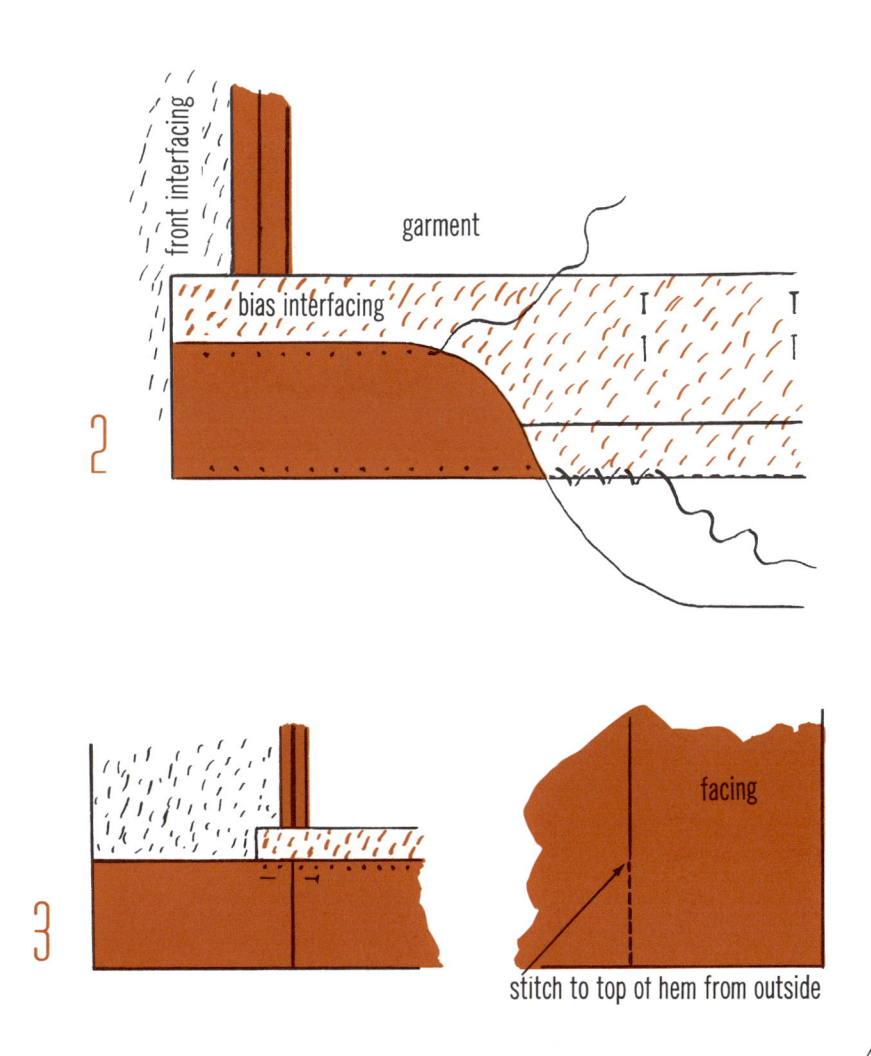

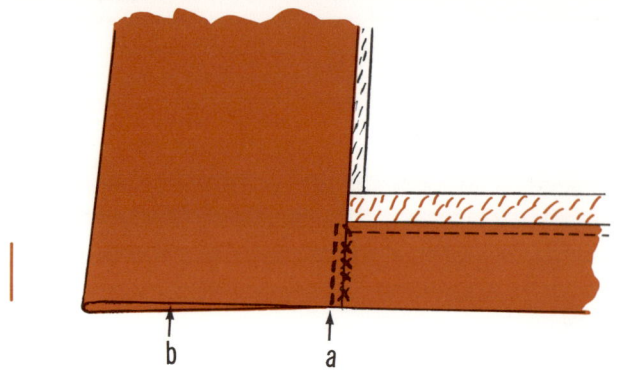

With a running stitch by hand, reach in and stitch hem of facings to hem of garment ½ inch (1.3cm) from edge. Grade under seam to ¼ inch (6mm). In soft woolens, you may also tack facing to hem halfway down width of hem. The stitching should be invisible in right side of facing.

At edge **a**, machine stitch the two raw edges — turned back facing and facing hem — together for reinforcement, trim any loose threads, and whipstitch facing to hem. Stitch through hem only, and do not catch interfacing or garment.

Leave bottom of facing open at **b**. This allows the facing to shape itself to the figure and form the lapel without pull or strain. The backs of finished buttonholes (page 89) may be whipstitched in place at this time; buttons may be sewn on (page 83).

Carefully and thoroughly final press the garment where needed at this time. (Final pressing cannot be done as well after lining is in, so do it now.) An excellent sequence is this: sleeves, shoulders, garment front, garment back, hem, collar, lapel, and facing unit.

Hang garment carefully on a wooden or padded hanger, and fasten one or more closings to keep it on grain while you proceed with the lining.

LINING

CUT LINING

If any pattern adjustments were necessary when cutting garment piece, cut the lining with the same alterations. If any fitting was necessary when the garment was tried on, cut and stitch the lining with those alterations.

When the garment has many cut details, such as yokes and applied seams, use the separate lining tissue (included with many patterns) so that the lining will be easier to manage. Otherwise, the pattern used for cutting the garment is generally preferred for cutting lining. The cutting and fitting alterations for the garment should already have been made and noted. If the following special directions for cutting are carried out, the lining will fit the garment with perfection.

Sleeves are cut precisely as for garment, except in length. Turn up the tissue pattern the width of the hem less 1 inch (2.5cm) before cutting the lining. This will permit you to cut the lining to the finished length of the garment sleeve plus 1 inch (2.5cm)

The front and back of lining are cut to the finished length for the jacket. If the jacket has a 1½-inch (3.8-cm) hem, turn up tissue pattern the depth of hem to cut lining. For a coat, the lining is cut to finished length plus 1 inch (2.5cm) for ease. This will give a deep takeup tuck in the finished lining.

One inch (2.5cm) of extra width is added at center back of lining for a pleat, **a**, to give necessary ease. If the pattern has a seam at the center back, cut additional lining for the pleat, **b**, at an angle, tapering to cutting line at waistline. (This cannot be done when the pattern shows a fold at center back because the lining would be off-grain.) On a coat with a full back a pleat in the lining is not necessary.

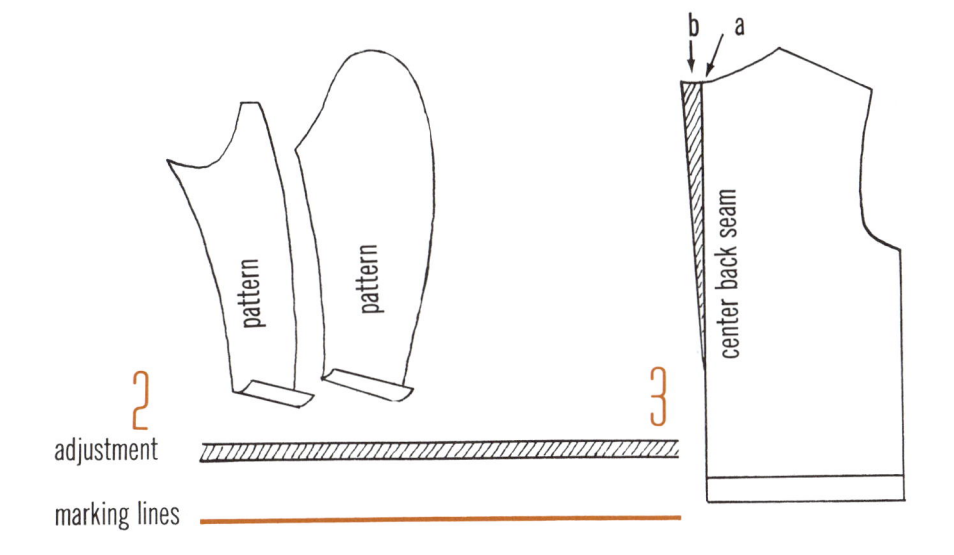

adjustment

marking lines

Mark with chalk on the jacket front pattern the width of front facing, line **c**. Measure 1¼ inches (3.2cm) — 2 seam-widths — from line **c** toward jacket front, and mark line **d** with chalk. Fold pattern under on line **d** to cut lining for jacket front. Repeat this procedure on jacket back, marking the neckline facing at line **e** and 1¼ inches (3.2cm) toward neckline, line **f**. Cut lining for jacket at neckline on line **f**.

Depending on how you prefer to finish the lining at the armholes after it has been inserted, you can cut on additional fabric at armholes of lining on one of two ways. To turn the body lining over the sleeve lining and finish it in the armhole, cut on 1½ inches (3.8cm) at armhole front and back, **g**, above notch, tapering to original cutting line at notch; add ¼ inch (6mm) extra height at shoulderline, **h**, as shown, starting at armhole and tapering to original cutting line about halfway to neckline. Also, cut on ½ inch (1.3cm) at underarms, **i**, tapering gradually to cutting line below underarm notch.

For the second method of attaching sleeve lining at armholes — turning the sleeve linings over the armholes (page 56) — cut the body lining at armholes as follows: Add ¼ inch (6mm) at shoulder seam, **h**, of armhole, tapering to original cutting line halfway to neckline; add the same amount at armhole on underarm seam, **i**, tapering to original cutting line a little below the underarm notch.

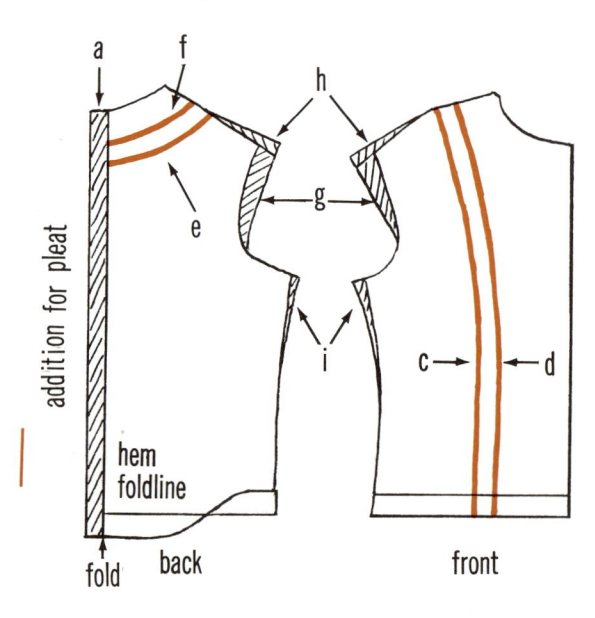

46

staystitching ....

basting — — — — — — — —

permanent stitching -- -- -- -- -- --

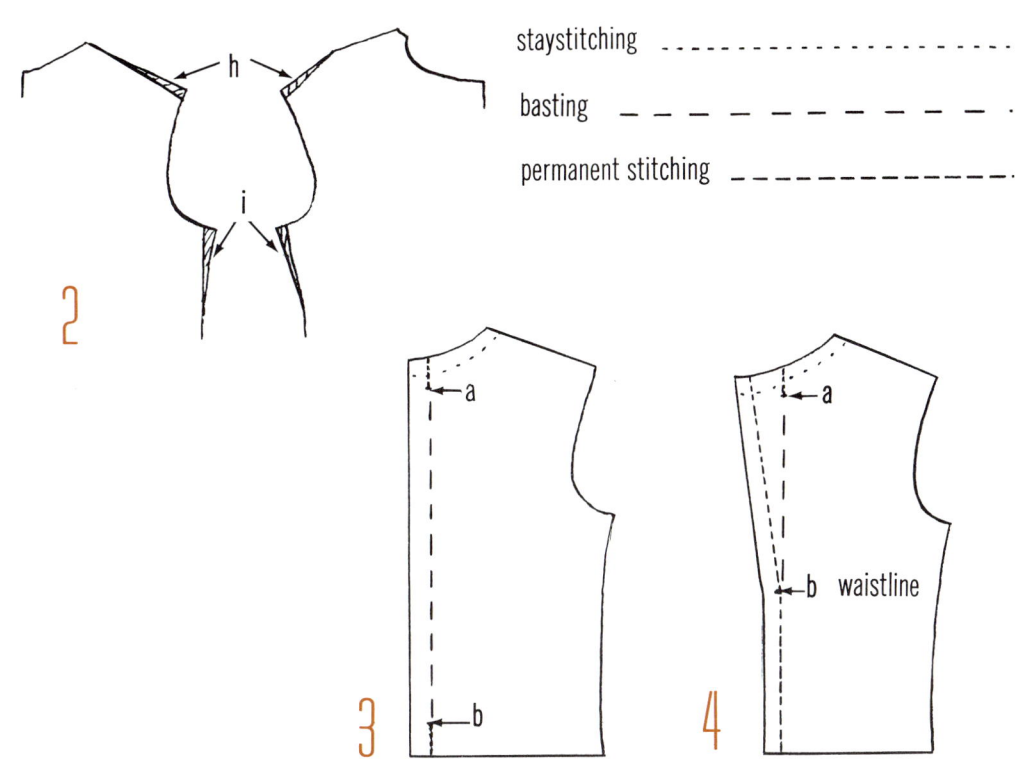

SEW LINING

The lining is staystitched only at the garment back neckline because the cut edges must be easy to mold. (This edge later is clipped to the staystitching.) Staystitch back neckline of lining on the ⅝-inch (1.5cm) seamline.

When there is no center back seam, stitch 1 inch (2.5cm) from center back fold: Use permanent stitches for 1½ inches (3.8cm) to point **a**; lockstitch. Continue stitching, using basting stitches to 1½ inches (3.8cm) from lower edge, **b**, of lining. Change to permanent stitch, lockstitch, and stitch to lower edge. Clip baste stitches at **a** and **b**, for easy removal of basting later.

The illustration shows stitching seam and pleat in garment with center back seam. Use permanent stitching to waistline, **b**. Lockstitch and baste to 1½ inches (3.8cm) from top, **a**. Lockstitch, change to permanent stitch, and stitch to neckline; lockstitch again. Stitch edges permanently from waist to neckline at ⅝ inch (1.5cm) as shown.

47

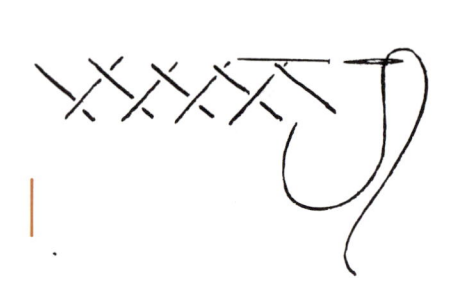

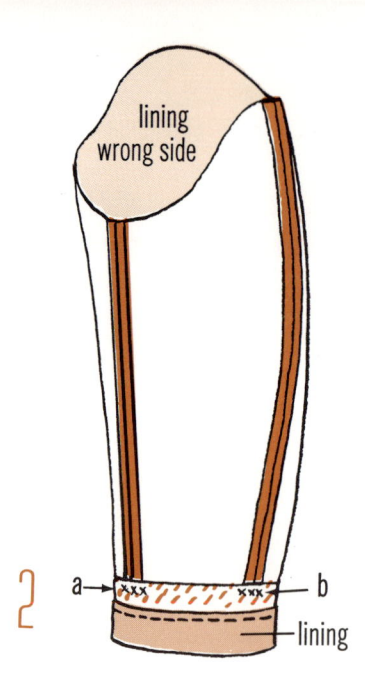

Lightly hand-baste pleat on fragile fabrics. Press pleat to right side, and stitch in position along the neck and lower edge. Catch-stitch across pleat to hold in place. Work from left to right, catching lining at the lower limit, then at the upper limit as shown.

Stitch lining together except at shoulder seams, and press all seams before sewing into garment. To give ease with a firm lining, stitch seams nearer ½ than ⅝ inch (1.3 than 1.5cm) except at lower edge. Here, make seams a little deeper than ⅝ inch (1.5cm).

Usually no steam is used to press lining. Steam, unless discreetly used, can easily give an overpressed look to the lining. Press seams open and darts in opposite direction from those in garment.

Sew and press the seams of the sleeve linings in the correct grain direction, but do not stitch the sleevecap at all. Sew sleeve seams a little less than ⅝ inch (1.5cm) at lower edge. Do not finish sleeve seams in lining or in garment. The lining can be sewn into the garment perfectly if the raw edges of both can be keyed together. Also, when seams are enclosed as with the garment and lining, they cannot rub against the body during wear, so seam finishing is unnecessary.

INSERT SLEEVE LINING

Slide the lining inside the sleeve with right sides together. Draw out bottom of lining, and turn it up to raw edge of the sleeve hem. Sew with a small running stitch or a machine stitch. Then catch-stitch interfacing at **a** and **b**. Hem is not sewn to sleeve at any other place.

Next, draw lining out of sleeve. Beginning about 2 inches (5cm) below armhole, attach one side of lining seam to the corresponding side of sleeve seam with a single thread and a long, easy running stitch through the middle of the seam allowance. Back-stitch several times at the beginning (even with a knot in the thread) and at the end of the stitching to secure the thread in fabric. Fasten the thread about 2 inches (5cm) above top of sleeve hem. Repeat for second seam of two-piece sleeve.

Draw the sleeve inside the lining. Press the excess lining at the bottom of the sleeve to form a take-up tuck. Many expensive garments feature a deep take-up tuck over hems in sleeves.

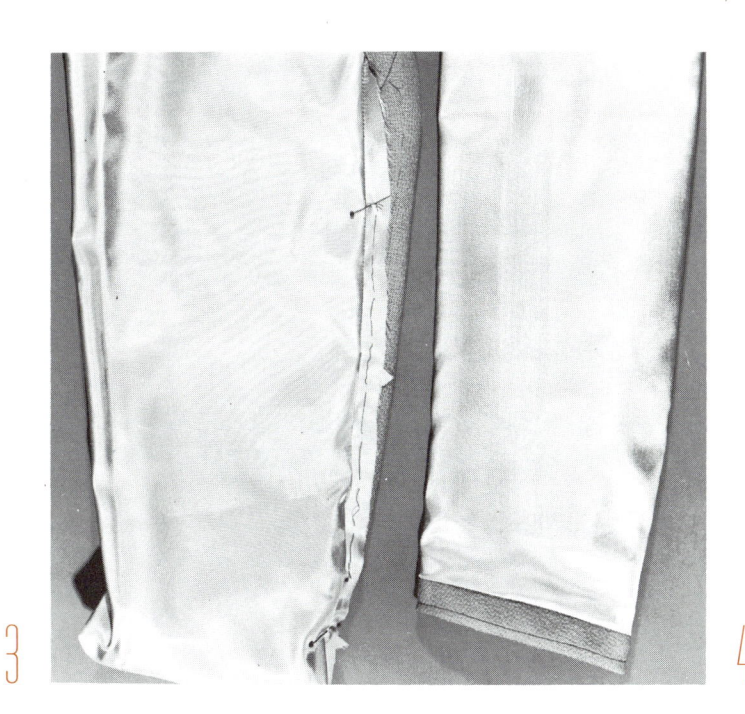

Match raw edges and key armhole of lining to armhole of sleeve at notches, underarm seam, and shoulder seam. With a loose running stitch, tack cap of lining to that of sleeve, easing in lining fullness over cap. Take small running stitches close to seam below notches. Trim seam (four thicknesses) to ¼ inch (6mm) under the arm between notches.

INSERT GARMENT LINING

Key lower edge of garment lining with lower edge of garment. Several inches above top of hem, align one pin in the lining and one in garment facing each other, as shown. These are called guide pins and will be used later to key these lower edges to perfection. Repeat on other side of garment.

Now place the lining and garment right sides together with lining extended downward as shown. With raw edge of the lining meeting raw edge of garment hem, pin at every seam. The raw edge of lining should be folded back ⅝ inch (1.5cm) at **a** and brought to staystitching on seamline at **b**. Then sew with a small running or machine basting stitch.

It is much easier to sew the lining to the hem by hand from underside or at the machine before doing hand hemming.

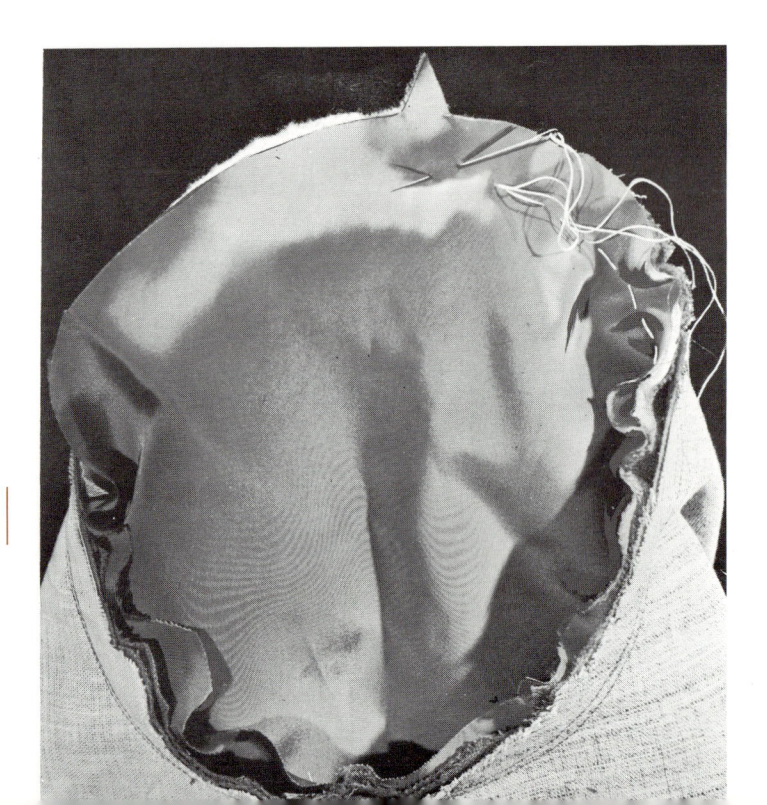

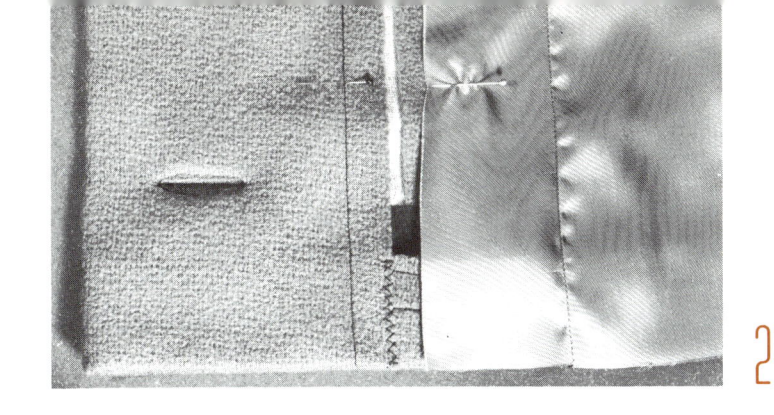

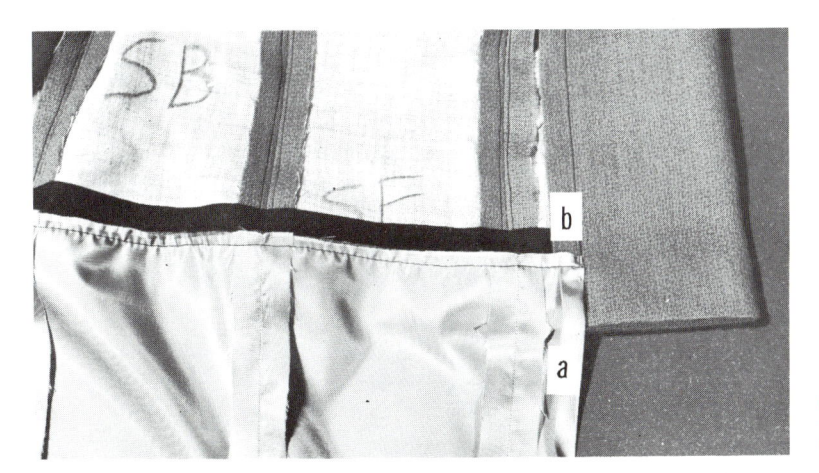

At this stage the garment should be hemmed by hand. Fold hem to outside of garment, and work from underside of hem, holding hem edge away from you, and garment toward you. With a single thread, hem with loose prick stitches ½ inch (1.3cm) apart. In one stitch, catch interfacing in hem; in the next, the garment.

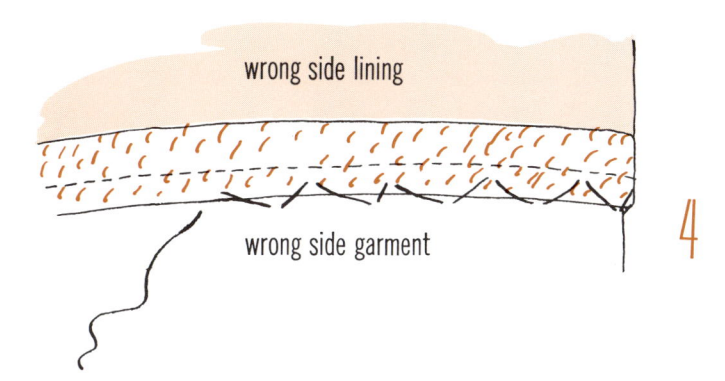

51

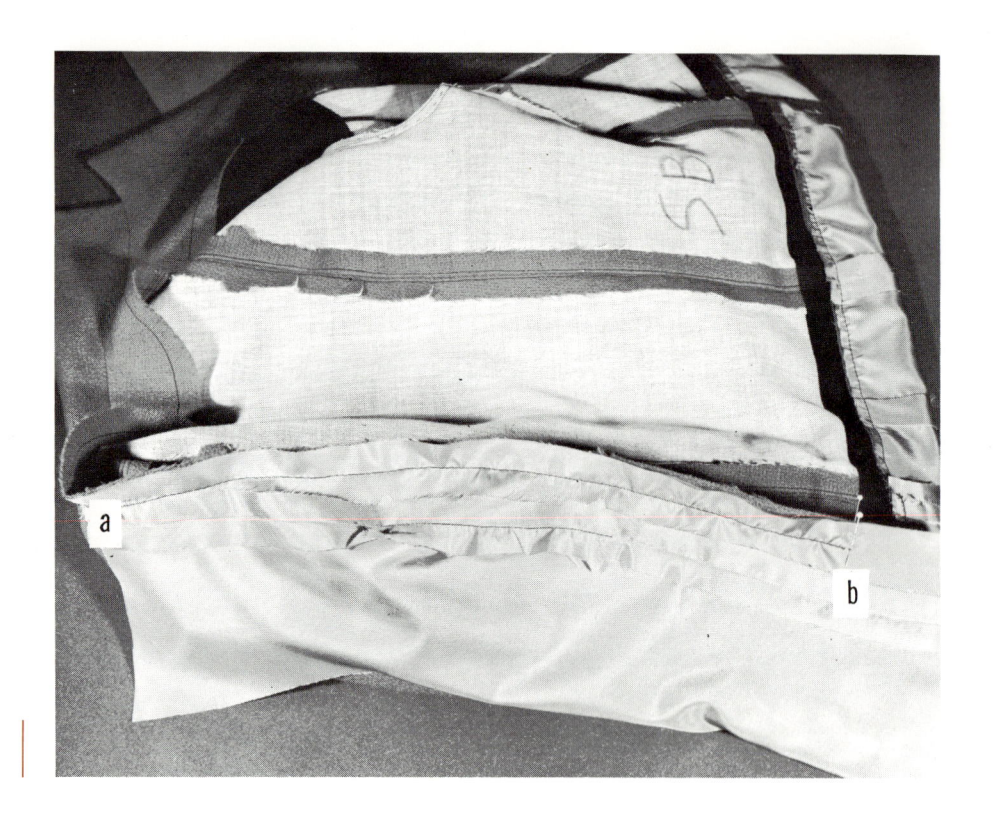

Key lining at the shoulders, and pin. The raw edge of lining will extend over shoulder seam of facing, **a**, ⅝ inch (1.5cm). Key lining to facing near lower edge, and pin together bringing two guide pins to meet, **b**. Repeat on other side of garment. Stitch the lining to the facings from guide pins to shoulder seam. Keep facing side up, and stitch one thread inside staystitching on facings seamlines. Use the longest stitch at the machine unless it puckers. If it does, shorten stitch slightly, or use a small running hand stitch. The extra inch cut on a coat lining is eased in here at this time.

Turn garment and lining to their correct positions — wrong sides together. There will be openings in the lining at lower edges of front facings. Press excess lining downward. This is known as a take-up tuck, which is necessary if lining is to wear well. Slipstitch lower edges of front facings and lining together. Include take-up

52

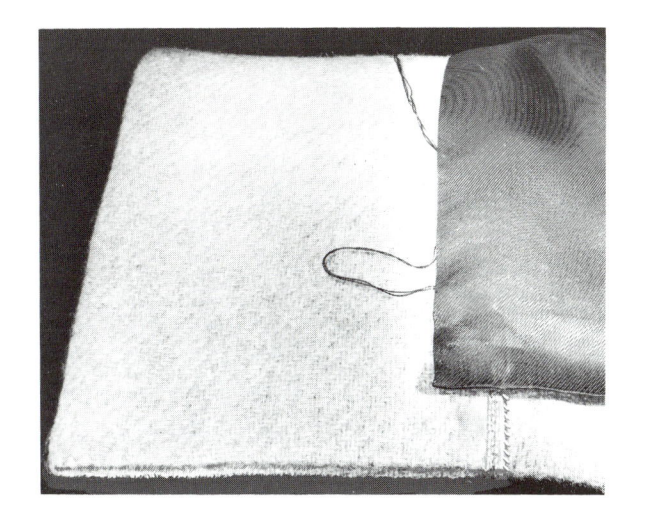

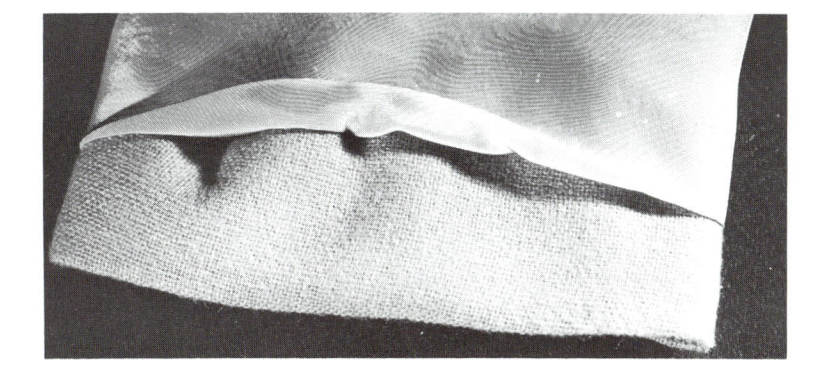

tuck to hold it in place. Press lining flat at front facings. One hallmark of quality is deep take-up tucks in sleeves and hem.

Tack one side of each lining seam allowance to the corresponding garment seam allowance. Begin and end stitching about 2 inches (5cm) from each end of seam. With a single thread, make a long, easy running stitch through the middle of the seam allowance as for sleeve linings, page 49. Make several back stitches at the beginning (even if the thread is knotted at the end). Do this at end of stitching to secure the thread in fabric.

Key raw shoulder edge of lining front to raw edge of back half of garment shoulder seam, **a**. Attach with an easy running stitch. Clip the back of the neckline on lining to staystitching, **b**. Turn under lining seam allowance at back of neckline and back shoulder seams, **c**. At back of neckline, you may trim seam allowance to ¼ inch (6mm).

Whipstitch in place using double thread, heavy duty thread, or buttonhole twist. It can be strengthened by running through beeswax and pressing with a warm iron before using it. The whipstitch is a firmer stitch than the slipstitch and is used where greater strength is needed. The amount of thread showing at the lining fold should be so small that stitches can scarcely be seen.

ARMHOLE, METHOD ONE

Place pins in body of the garment, **a**, so you do not draw lining; then pin at armholes as shown. Below notches at armhole, **b**, turn in lining ⅛ inch (3mm); clip curve when necessary. Lap body lining over sleeve lining ¼ inch (6mm), and pin in place. Above notches, turn in lining to lap over seam **c**, after turning raw edge under ¼ inch (6mm). Pin in place. If all of the extra 1½ inches (3.8cm) cut on is not needed, cut away excess before turning under and pinning raw edge. Hold the garment in such a way that armhole seam is toward you. One of the secrets of this method is holding the garment carefully. Whipstitch the lining around armholes in the same way as for shoulders and back facing, preceding paragraph.

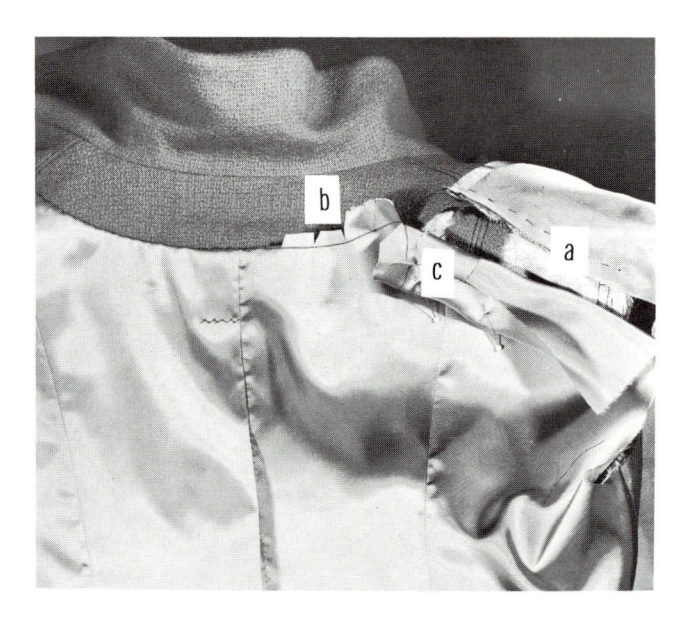

2

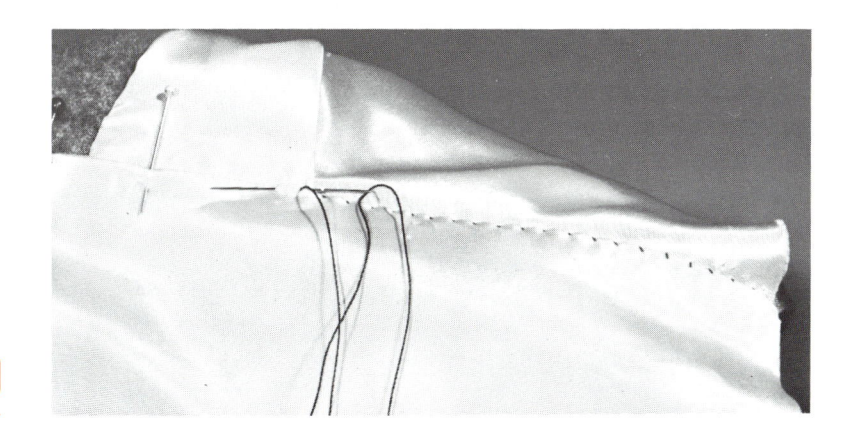

3
a
b
c

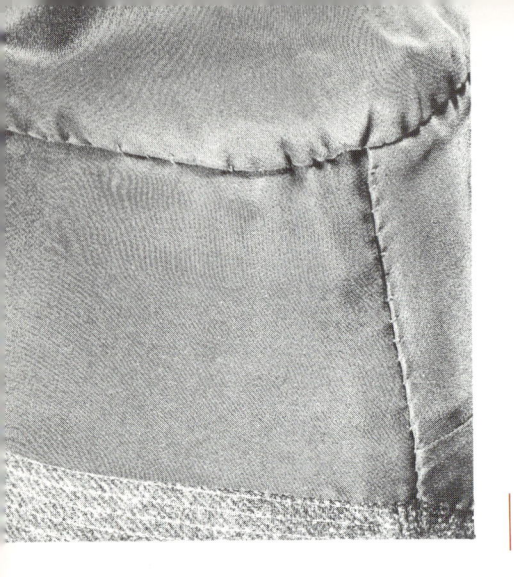

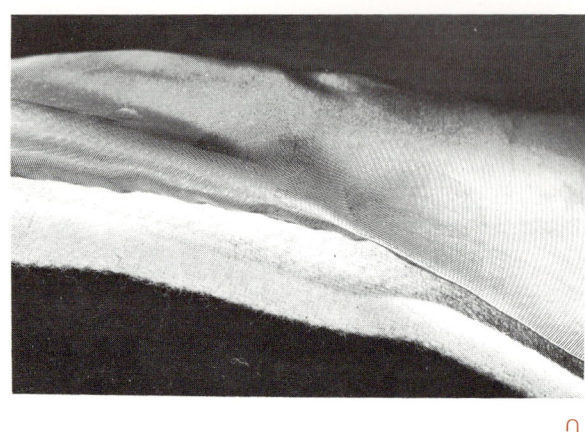

ARMHOLE, METHOD TWO
If you cut lining for this method [adding ¼ inch (6mm) at shoulder seam and at underarm edge—page 46] proceed as follows: Sew garment lining to armhole with a running stitch ¼ inch (6mm) from edge; underarm, stitch it near seamline. The ¼ inch (6mm) added at shoulders and underarm gives some ease. Trim all of the seam allowances to ¼ inch (6mm) underarm between notches.

Stitch an ease line on sleevecap ¼ inch (6mm) from edge. Draw up thread to ease fullness in cap. Fasten thread, and turn raw edge under on stitching line. Lap sleeve cap over armhole ¼ inch (6mm); whipstitch in place.

Remove the baste-stitching in the back pleat. If the outer fabric has become wrinkled from the handling as the lining was being attached, some light final pressing of garment may be necessary again. Do not press lining at shoulders, back neckline, and around armholes.

CUT-ON SLEEVES
The only difference in inserting a lining with cut-on sleeves is that the body of the lining is done first with steps already shown. The very last step is to finish the bottom of the sleeves. Turn under raw edge of lining ¼ inch, and pin ¼ inch from raw edge of sleeve hem. Slipstitch by hand. Lightly press in take-up tuck.

SIMPLE TAILORING FOR KNITS
AND NON-WOOL FABRICS

The use of fusibles as interfacings is recommended only for polyester double knits, wool knits, cottons, and some blends.

This section shows how to cut and apply fusibles and gives other information pertinent to simple tailoring. Refer to the preceding section, Couture Tailoring, for the complete steps to make your garment.

Fusibles come in various weights. Determine the best choice for the weight of your fabric. Carefully read the directions accompanying your purchase for information on cutting, grain direction, and for the application — steam, heat, pressure, and use of press cloth. After application it is of utmost importance not to remove fabric from the ironing board until it is cool.

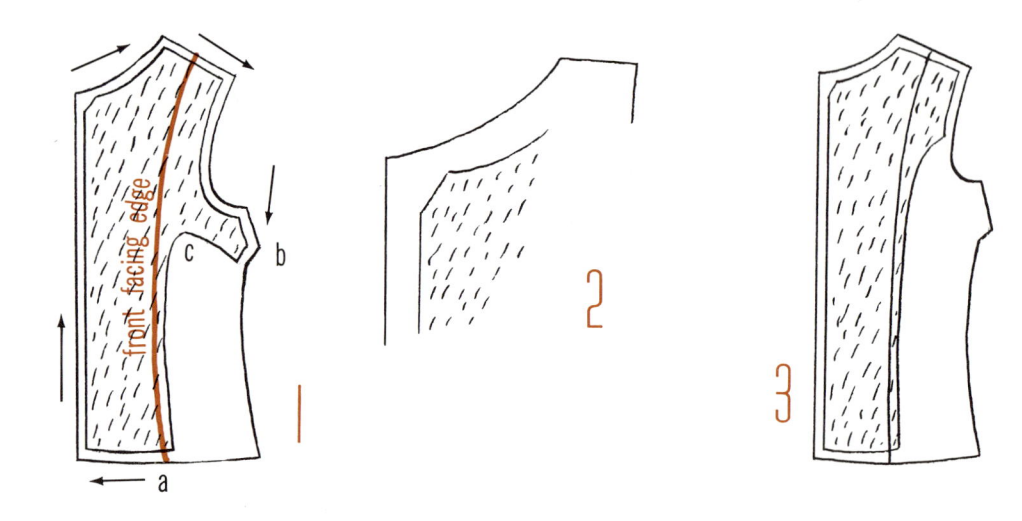

CUTTING AND APPLYING INTERFACING

GARMENT FRONT INTERFACING

Unless the pattern company has given separate pattern pieces for interfacing exactly like those described in directions to follow, use the original pattern pieces to cut the interfacing. Cut it on the same grain as the garment.

Garment front interfacing is cut exactly like the pattern from point **a** around to **b**, which is approximately 2 inches (5cm) below the armhole. With tracing paper and tracing wheel, mark center front, buttonholes, and any darts. Remove tissue. Key pattern for front facing in place on top of interfacing. Continue cutting ¼ inch (6mm) wider than front facing as far as bustline, **c**. Then swing out and cut freehand to meet point **b**.

Try a sample and if the fusible interfacing forms a ridge at the inside edge when pressed in place on fabric, pink the inside edges first. This will apply to all inside edges of fusible interfacings.

Trim ½ inch (1.3cm) from seam allowance; the other ⅛ inch (3mm) will be caught in the seams when they are stitched. At point of lapel cut off corner of interfacing ¼ inch (6mm) inside the seamline to reduce bulk in corner.

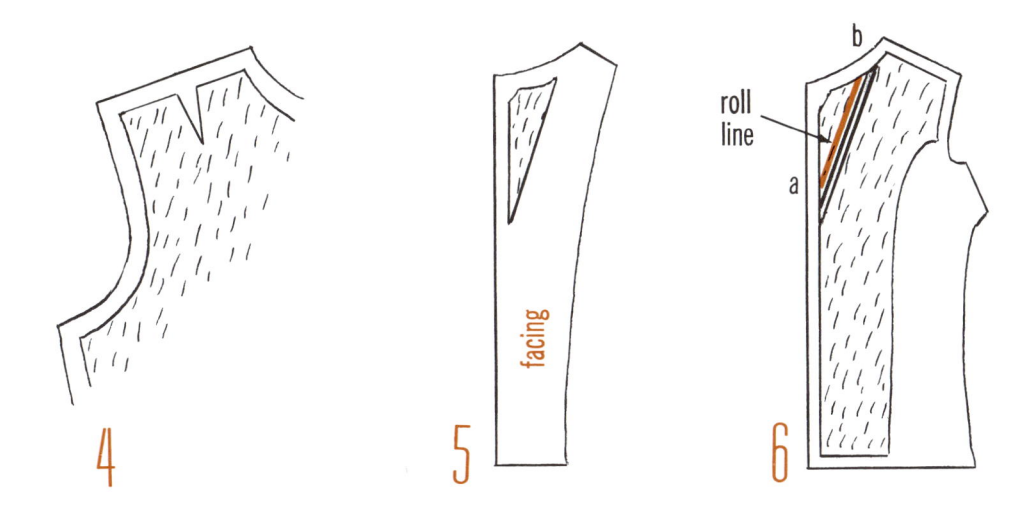

If a knit jacket will not be lined, just cut the interfacing to extend halfway down the armhole. Then cut the front facing exactly the same shape to conceal interfacing.

Cut darts away a good ⅛ inch (3mm) beyond their marking lines. After interfacing is pressed in place, the darts can be stitched without catching interfacing in stitching line.

If you feel the front lapel needs a little more support, cut a second piece of interfacing to extend to roll line of lapel. Press it on the wrong side of facing.

ROLL LINE

Depending upon the weight of your knit, you may want to tape the roll line of your lapel to further stabilize it and prevent this edge from stretching and losing its shape as a result of wear, laundering, or cleaning.

Cut a piece of PRESHRUNK twill tape to extend from the shoulder seam at the neckline edge to the point where the lapel roll begins. Press on top of interfacing with a ¼-inch (6-mm) wide strip of fusible tape. Be sure it is not included in seamlines at **a** and **b**. Place it ¼ inch (6mm) from the roll line toward the body of the garment.

INTERFACING FOR FOLDBACK FRONT FACING
If the pattern for your garment has a foldback facing, or if you wish to cut one on (see page 66), cut the interfacing precisely like those preceding with this exception: extend it only to foldline of facing unless you feel the front edge needs a little more support. If so, cut a ½-inch (1.3-cm) strip and press it in place over original interfacing.

GARMENT BACK INTERFACING
Back interfacing is cut exactly like the pattern for garment back from **a**, 3 to 5 inches (7.5 to 12.5cm) down the center back—around to **b**, 2 inches (5cm) below the armhole. Mark back shoulder darts with tracing paper and wheel. Remove pattern and cut freehand from **a** to **b**. Trim ½ inch (1.3cm) from seam allowance; the other ⅛ inch (3cm) will be caught in the seams when they are stitched. Usually the fusible in the back shoulders is of a lighter weight than that used in front.

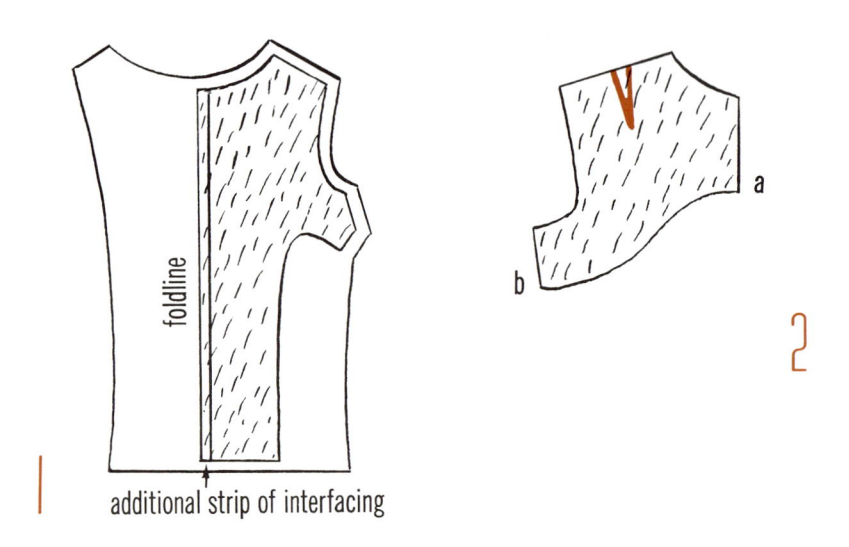

additional strip of interfacing

If the knit jacket will not be lined, cut the back interfacing just to extend halfway down the armhole; then cut the back facing exactly the same way. The back facing can be seamed separately to front facing at shoulders, but it will be stitched in armhole seams.

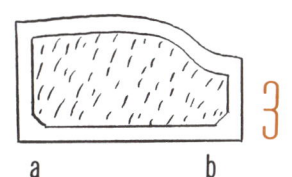

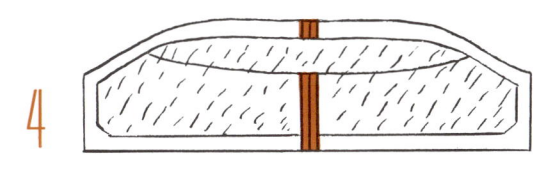

Cut darts away a good ⅛ inch (3mm) beyond their marking lines. Then, when interfacing is pressed in place, the darts can be stitched without catching interfacing.

Fuse interfacing to fabric according to manufacturer's directions. Fuse it to each piece of the garment before seams are stitched.

EXTRA INTERFACING IN SHOULDERS
When fitting your garment, if the shoulder area needs support anywhere, extra layers of interfacing can be pressed on, as shown for lapels, page 59.

COLLAR
Cut interfacing exactly as you did the under collar. Trim ½ inch (1.3cm) from seam allowances, and cut off corners **a** and **b** ¼ inch (6mm) inside seamline to reduce bulk. Apply to under collar according to manufacturer's directions.

If the collar needs a little more support at the roll line, cut a second interfacing piece that will extend from roll line of collar to seamline of neck edge. Eliminate center back seam in this piece, and

fabric	fabric wrong side
underlining	
interfacing either side	interfacing either side
interlining either side	
lining	lining wrong side

61

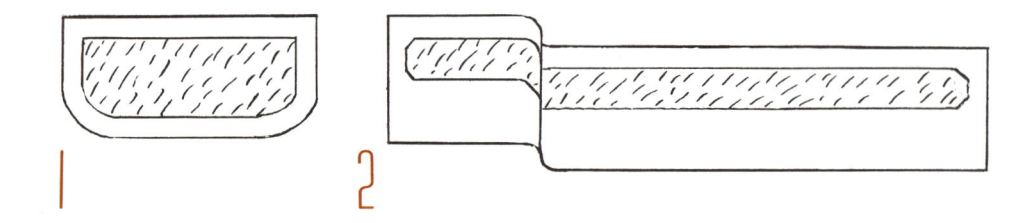

cut on true bias. Apply over first layer of interfacing after under collar is joined at center back. This collar will be shaped on a cushion as on page 35.

POCKETS
On seams that are to be trimmed and turned, trim ¾ inch (2cm) from interfacing, so it will not be caught in the seams. Apply to underside of pocket flap or welt.

WAISTBANDS AND BELTS
Cut interfacing half the width of the band or belt. Trim ½ inch (1.3cm) from seam allowances, and cut off corners of interfacing ¼ inch (6mm) inside seamline to reduce bulk when turned. When pressing in position, place one edge along foldline. Apply according to directions.

HEMS
When you have determined the length of garment or sleeves, turn up and press hem. Use staystitch plus or easing to remove fullness at top of hem where necessary. Cut bias strips of interfacing ½ inch (1.3cm) wider than hem allowance. If garment will not be lined, cut interfacing the width of the hem. Position interfacing on hem, one edge on foldline; press in place. Place under, not over, seam allowance. When ready to attach the hem, use a ¼-inch (6-mm) strip of fusible hem tape placed just under edge of hem. Pin it just inside the edge of hem so it will not slip out of position. Remove pins just as you set iron on hem.

A strip of aluminum foil on press board will help heat to penetrate and melt fusible tape to hold hem in place. Test your fabric, however, before using the fusible tape. It does not hold well on some fabrics.

BUTTONHOLES

Buttonholes for quickly done knit garments are often made on the machine. A notion for making tailored buttonholes is another time saver. It works especially well on knits and makes buttonholes of good quality. Remember that backs of the tailored buttonholes on knits do not need to be finished. Simply cut the openings the desired size and whipstitch raw edge in place.

LINING

If you want to completely line your knit garment, follow the directions on pages 44–49. However, for simple tailoring, you have two other choices. One is to line the body of the garment but not the sleeves. The raw edges of the armholes can be whipstitched together to finish, or they can be bound with a piece of lining cut on the bias.

Another shortcut is to line only the front of the garment. It is done precisely as shown in the lining section except that the lining ends at, and is fastened to, the underarm seam.

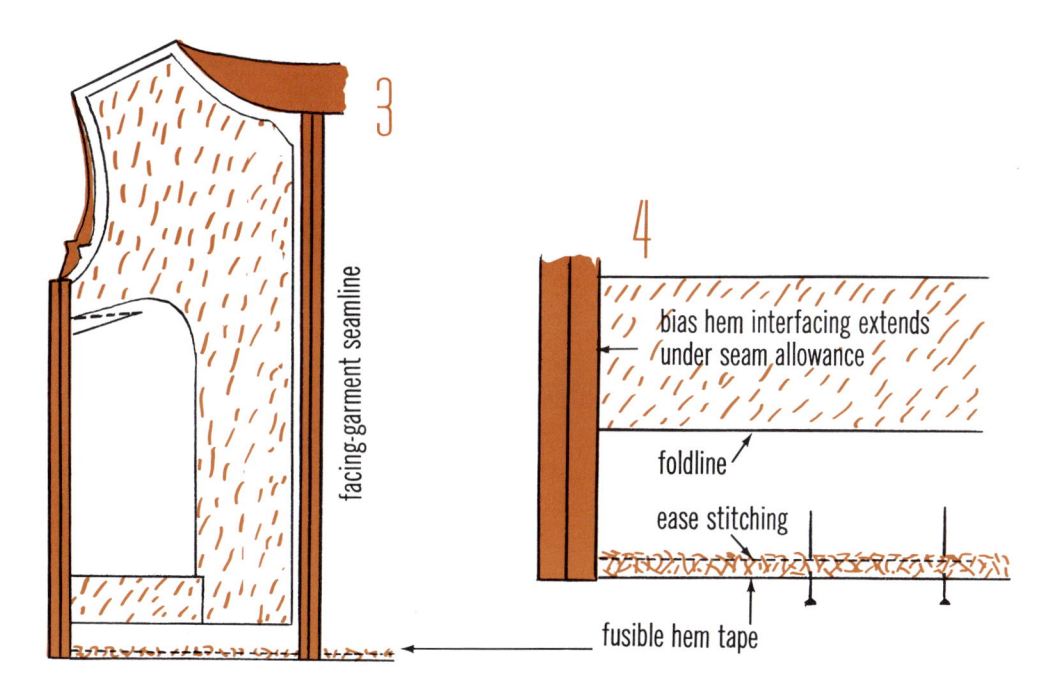

OTHER TAILORING TECHNIQUES

SHOULDER SHAPES

Shoulder shapes can be as individual as the person who makes them. Analyze your shoulders. Do you need larger shapes to make your shoulders more square, or small ones just to firm the outer edges of the garment shoulders? The shapes may be larger in front than back, or larger on one shoulder than another — they are made to conceal your fitting problems at the shoulders and should be placed in the garment at the time of fitting.

For a perfect fit, cut them from the same pattern as the garment. Pin front and back pattern pieces together at the shoulder seamlines. The standard size is 1 inch (2.5cm) from the neck edge and the same amount between the front and back notches at the armholes. Cut desired size for individual.

Cut four bias pieces for covers. Use a washable or dry-cleanable interfacing for garment, according to care you will give garment. Cut at least three graduated layers of polyester fleece for each shape. Make each succeeding layer ½ inch (1.3cm) smaller than the preceding on the outside edge.

Quilt the layers together with hand stitches, building or molding a curve or shape into pad as you stitch. The widest layer is on the bottom. Press and further mold the shoulder shape on the side of a cushion, and leave it there to cool. Pin shapes into garment for a fitting. To sew in place, tack by hand to shoulder and armhole seams and also to interfacing, front and back, if possible. Key shape to meet the edge of armhole seam.

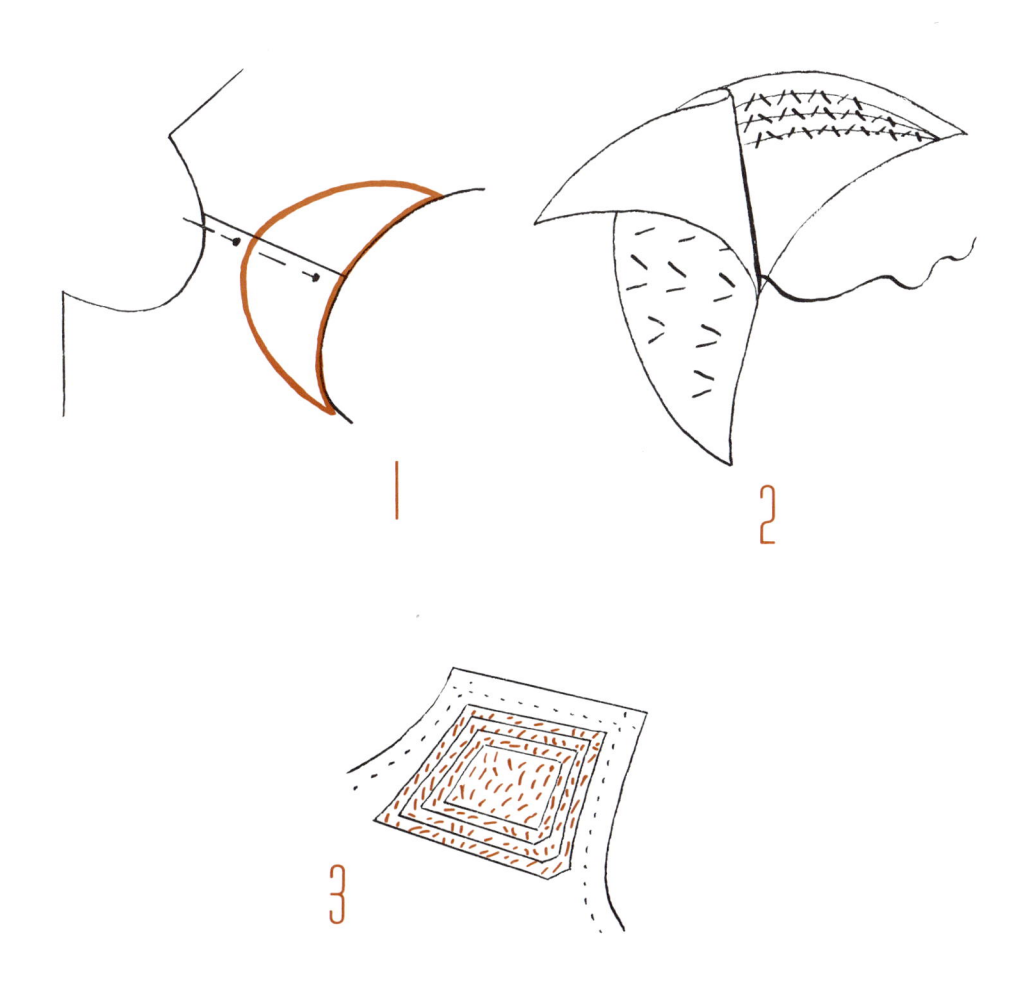

EXTRA INTERFACING AT SHOULDERS
When you are fitting a garment, add extra layers of interfacing anywhere they are needed to support a particular fabric or pattern line or to conceal a figure problem.

Simply cut graduated layers to be placed inside seamlines of a stitch-on or press-on interfacing. Suggestions for stitched-on interfacing are pellon, lambswool, flannel, polyester fleece. Press-on interfacings can be used the same way. Stitch extra layers to interfacing of garment.

65

FOLDBACK FACING

If the pattern you have chosen for your garment has a separate front facing, as this sketch illustrates, you can key and lap the seamlines of the front facing and garment front and pin the tissue together as shown. Then cut the facing together with front. This is especially desirable in heavy fabrics, but it cannot be done if the pattern calls for a shaped lapel unless the lapel line is straightened.

If you would like a wider lap on the front of your garment, especially if you want to use very large buttons, bring **a** cutting line to meet **b** cutting line. It would then be cut as one, but with the ⅝-inch (1.5-cm) seam allowances at foldline added to front width.

INTERFACING

CUTTING INTERFACING FOR FOLDBACK FACING

There are three ways to cut the interfacing:

1. With lightweight garments and stitched interfacings, the interfacing can be cut to extend all the way to the edge of the facings.
2. If the front edge needs reinforcement, but you do not want to extend interfacing all the way to the edge of the facing, cut it to extend 1 inch (2.5cm) beyond the folded edge of facing. This will only be possible when working with interfacing that creases well at the fold.
3. Cut interfacing to extend to foldline only (see page 60) if you are using fusible interfacing.

FOLDBACK FACING WITH INTERFACING BEYOND FOLD

With a running stitch, mark by hand the foldline of the facing so that it will show on right side of fabric.

Then place interfacing on underside of garment front and pin it. Turn garment right side up, and stitch interfacing in place at foldline with a prick stitch on outside and ¼-inch (6-mm) running stitch on underside. The hand stitch should be invisible on the right side. See two preceding illustrations.

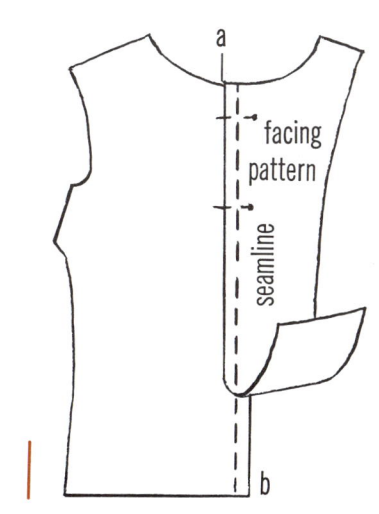

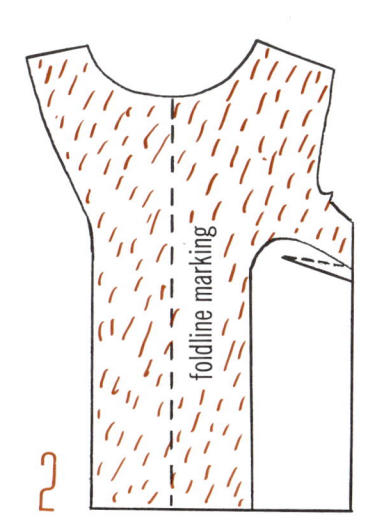

The next step is to press the front facings back on the foldline. They should lie in place with absolute grain perfection, not only at the front, but at neckline, shoulder, and hem edges as well.

ATTACHING REGULAR INTERFACING TO FOLDBACK FACING
Place a strip of rayon seam binding or twill tape along the entire front edge of interfacing such as hair canvas, lapping edge of tape and edge of hair canvas. With tape side turned up, stitch tape and interfacing together ¼ inch (6mm) from edge; stitch again on inside of tape. Press if necessary.

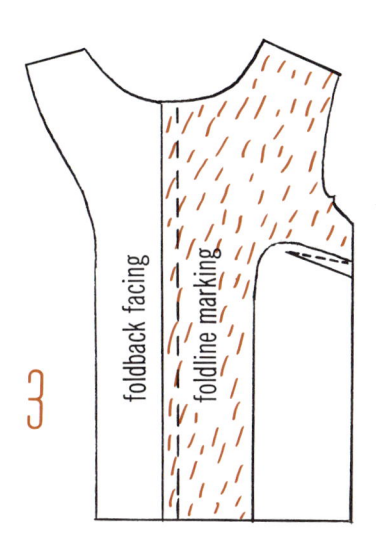

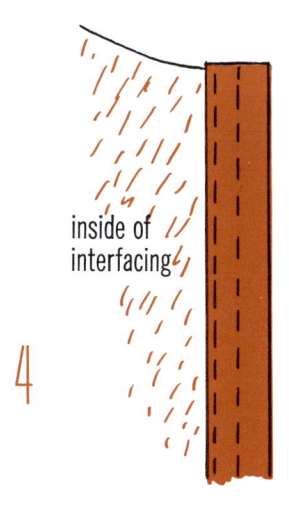

The marking line for foldline will be on underside. Use a row of baste stitches to mark it on outside. Press facing back perfectly on foldline.

Lay interfacing on underside of garment front, and fasten to fold of garment with running stitch along the edge of the tape. Stitches should be ⅜ inch (1cm) long on underside and only prick through fold of garment; they must be invisible on the right side.

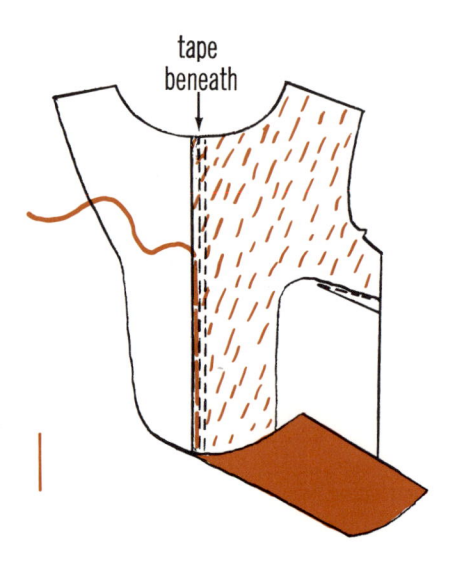

tape beneath

UNDERLINING AND INTERFACING

Choose underlining as discussed on page 8. The underlining is cut precisely as the garment with the same tissue.

Center front and buttonhole locations are marked on underlining only, unless an interfacing is used as well. If you have made a trial garment, permanent-stitch darts in garment and underlining separately before joining them. Or baste garment pieces and fit darts before proceeding with underlining construction.

When two layers of fabric are stitched together, the one on the outside must be slightly larger to turn and finish smoothly over the under layer. This is called the turn-of-the-cloth principle. To insure that the garment fabric will lie smoothly over underlining, use the following procedure.

Place a section of the outer fabric on the press board, wrong side up. Press out any wrinkles and creases, pressing with the grain. Lay corresponding piece of underlining, marked side up, on the garment piece. Press it smooth, again pressing on grain.

Note how the two fabrics work together. Pin them together along the center line, parallel to the lengthwise grain. Next key and pin edges at shoulders, neckline, and armholes. Place pins inside seamline at right angles to edge. Below the armhole the layers must be turned before pinning to allow for the turn-of-the-cloth. Fold or roll the two layers, on the lengthwise grain, toward the center of the garment.

Carefully smooth out the excess underlining toward the side seam allowance. Pin the two layers together. The amount of slippage will vary depending upon the combination of the two fabrics. On lightweight fabrics there may be none at all.

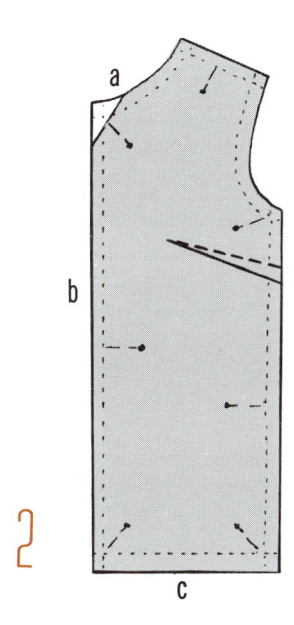

Staystitch edges **a** and **b** on the seamline. (This is where the collar and facing will be attached; the underlining can be trimmed away more easily.) The layers are more easily managed with the firm underlining on top. Hem edge, **c**, is staystitched ¾ inch (2cm)

from the edge. On a 1½-inch (3.8-cm) hem, underlining will turn up inside the hem half the hem width. Other edges are staystitched just outside seamline.

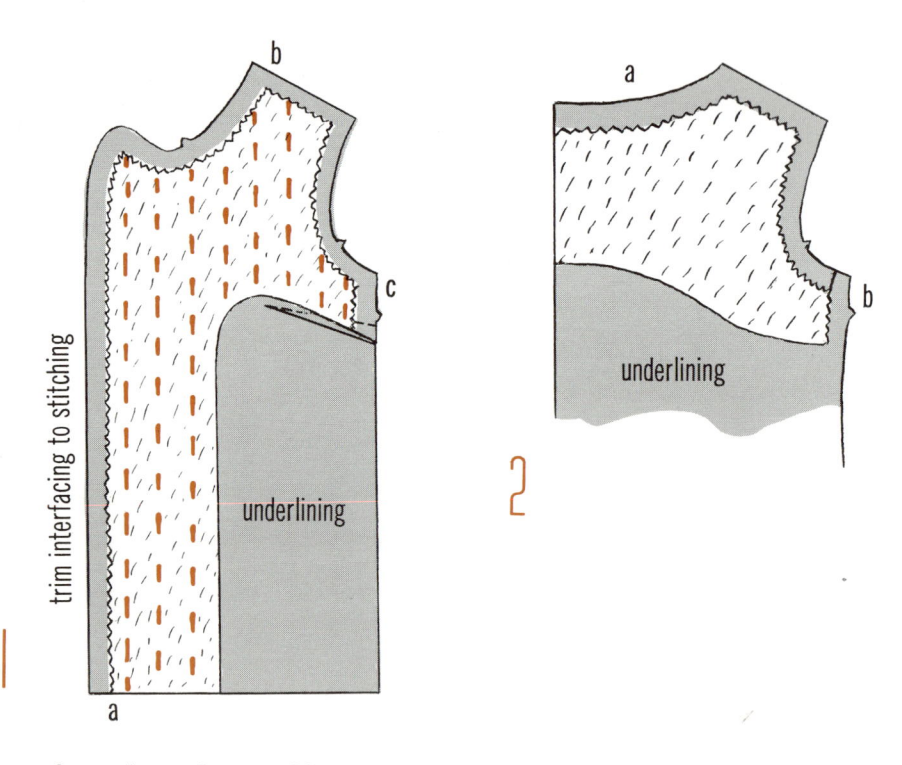

At lapel, trim corners of underlining away ¼ inch (6mm) inside the seamline. This is done at all corners to reduce bulk.

If an interfacing is needed in addition to lightweight underlining, cut according to instructions, page 15. Key edges of underlining and interfacing to match perfectly. Stitch interfacing to underlining before underlining is staystitched to garment. Use a

staystitching ....

basting   — — — — — — — — — — —

permanent stitching _____

zigzag stitching 〰〰〰〰〰〰〰〰〰〰〰

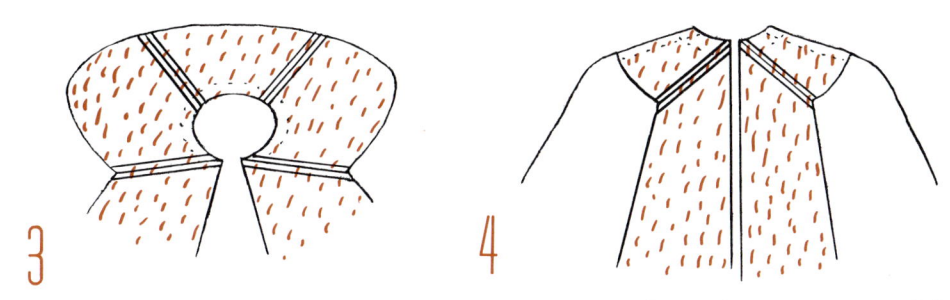

wide zigzag stitch (straight stitch if your machine has no zigzag) 1 inch (2.5cm) from edges **a** and **b** and ¾ inch (2cm) from **b** to **c**. Trim interfacing to stitch line. Machine or hand baste at 1½-inch (3.8-cm) intervals through interfacing and underlining.

Interfacing for the back is cut exactly as shown on page 17. Zigzag or straight-stitch to underlining 1 inch (2.5cm) from edge at **a** and ¾ inch (2cm) from other edges. Trim interfacing out to stitching at **a** and **b**, and staystitch underlining to garment.

INTERFACING FOR CUT-ON SLEEVES OR CAPES

For capes and for jackets and coats that have cut-on sleeves, interfacing is cut to extend from the neck edge as far out as the shoulder. If there are several pieces in the pattern, cut the interfacing the same as garment, and seam the sections of garment and interfacing separately. The finished side of interfacing will face the underside of garment, and the two will be staystitched together at neckline and shoulder. Staystitch at ⅝ inch (1.5cm) at neckline and ½ inch (1.3cm) at shoulders.

fabric	fabric wrong side
underlining	
interfacing either side	interfacing either side
interlining either side	
lining	lining wrong side

CURVED SEAM WITH UNDERLINING

To give real character to this seam and for a trim fit over the bustline, it is best to underline the front of the garment, unless the weight of the fabric will carry this line.

PIECING FABRIC AND INTERFACING

When you are short of fabric — sections for front facing and under cuff, for example — it can be pieced where it will not be seen. To piece fabric, stitch a ¼-inch (6-mm) seam and press open. The pieces must be cut and stitched together on exactly the same grain. Topstitch seam each side of seamline, and trim seam allowance to topstitching. Always piece the fabric before cutting out section of garment.

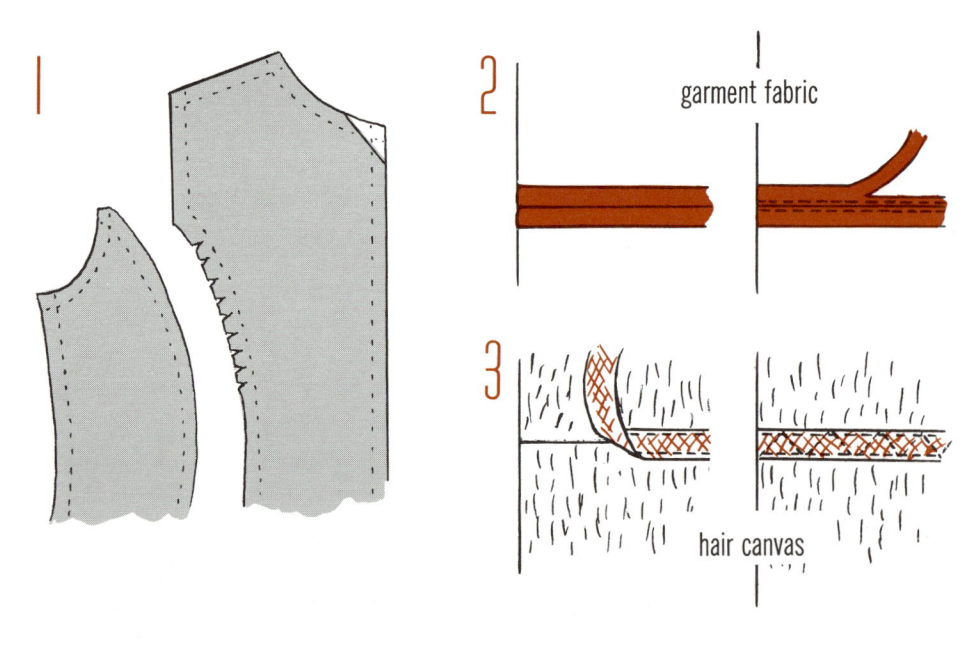

Hair canvas interfacing should not be seamed because a seam will leave a mark on outside of the garment when garment is pressed (unless it lies under a garment seam). Butt edges of interfacing, and apply a piece of seam tape. Stitch at both edges of tape, and stitch back and forth across tape to keep the butted edges of interfacing flat. The pieces butted together must be on the same grain. Always piece the interfacing before cutting out interfacing section, and place side of the interfacing with tape on it next to garment.

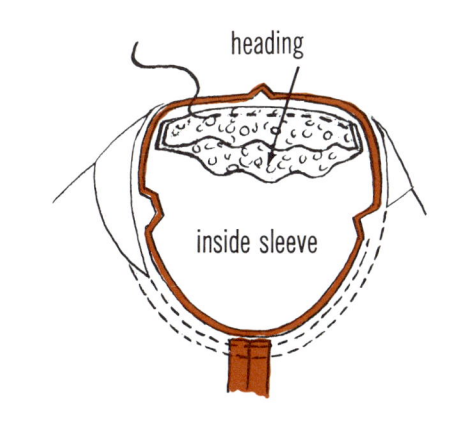

SLEEVE HEADS

Besides the shoulder shapes or pads, sleeve headings help to maintain a firm rounded look at the sleeve cap, especially in soft fabrics. Use strips of polyester fleece, flannelette, lamb's wool or other soft fabric. Cut them on bias 6 to 8 inches (15 to 20.5cm) long —depending on size of garment and texture of fabric—and 3 inches (7.5cm) wide. The heading may extend from notch to notch, or it may give a better line if it begins about 1 inch (2.5cm) above notch on each side. Fold lengthwise, leaving one edge extending 1 inch (2.5cm) beyond the other; press or stitch if necessary to hold. The ends may need to be tapered into curves. Stitch by hand as close as possible to seamline of sleeve, keeping wider side toward sleeve. (It is not necessary to stitch through all seam allowances.) Turn the armhole seam allowances into the sleeve before pressing.

TOPSTITCHING

Topstitching is not only a nice detail, it also serves to finish and/or to hold a finish on the edges of soft fabrics. An example is polyester knit, where topstitching not only holds the press but also helps to hold this resilient fabric in place. Topstitching also helps to flatten heavy tweeds. Areas to be topstitched should be pressed and pounded with the pounding block as professionally as possible before beginning to topstitch.

The presser foot or seam guide works beautifully in stitching on the edge and/or back a distance from it. Hand basting works on curves where it is difficult to use the seam guide accurately. If you are topstitching seams within the garment, a commercial adhesive tape that will serve as a guide is available. Another method is to tape a straight pin or half of a hair clip on the front of the regular presser foot. It should be placed the correct distance from the needle to gauge the desired space between topstitching and the seamline. Fasten with two small strips of masking tape. This is excellent for topstitching seams within the garment.

Topstitching will have more importance if you use heavy duty thread, a contrasting color, or even buttonhole twist, instead of regular thread on top of the machine. Heavier thread will require a larger needle — 14 to 16 — a looser top tension, and a longer stitch. Use regular thread in your bobbin.

Try a sample to decide what width of topstitching and how many rows will look best and hold fabric edges to perfection.

A row on the edge and a second row ¼ inch (6mm), ⅜ inch (1cm), or ½ inch (1.3cm) from it are all excellent choices.

If your fabric will not take a row on the edge attractively, try just one row back ¼ inch (6mm), ⅜ inch (1cm), or ½ inch (1.3) from the edge.

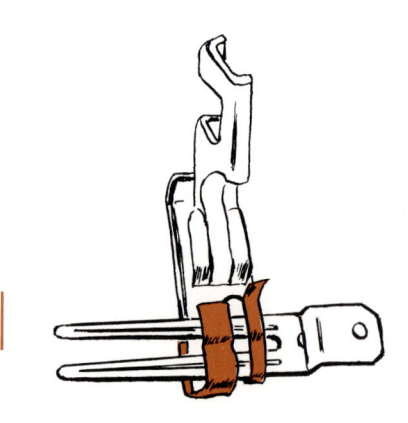

If garment edges are thick and wiry, sometimes three or four rows ⅛ to ¼ inch (3 to 6mm) apart will help to obtain thinner, sharper edges.

On large garments — coats with wide lapels, large collars, pockets, for example — topstitching may be especially attractive ¾ to 1 inch (2 to 2.5cm) from the edges.

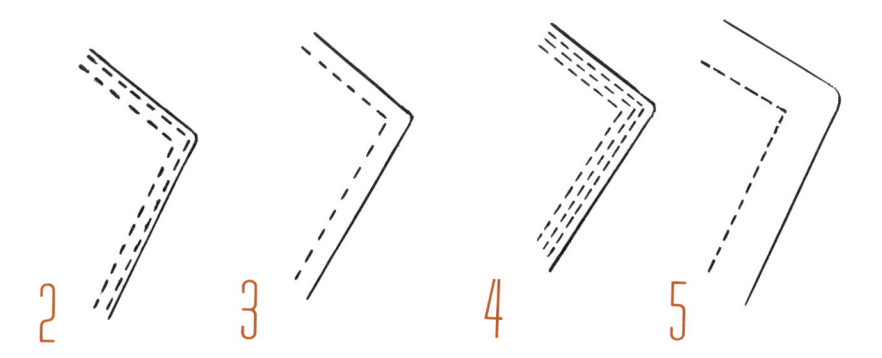

Topstitching that continues onto the lapel from the collar makes a garment look homemade. The couturiere way to do this is to continue topstitching in well of seam, **b,** if possible. If it is not easy to do, end topstitching at end of collar, **a**; then begin topstitching at end of lapel, **c.** The topstitching should always slant in the same direction as the edge of collar, **d,** or of lapel.

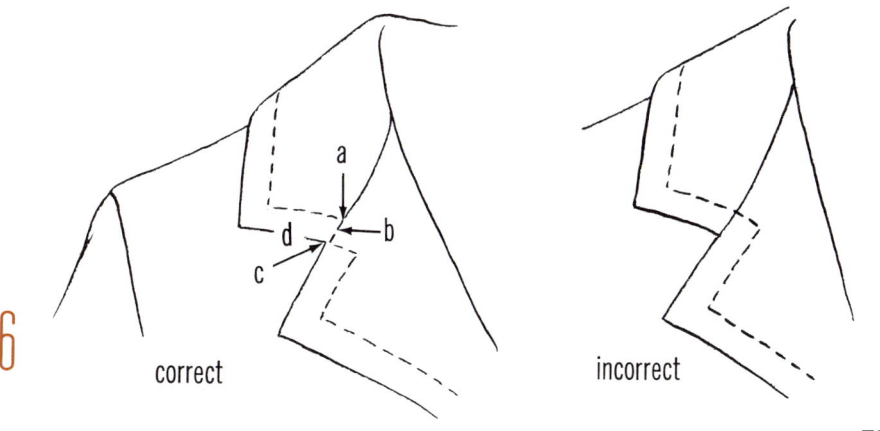

correct incorrect

1. Consider the possibility of topstitching with a longer stitch; then, using embroidery floss or buttonhole twist, outline the topstitching for a special detail. A couturiere touch is to unravel wool threads from garment fabric and use them for handstitching the detail.

2. Another couturiere touch is to use a chainstitch over the topstitching. Two or three rows spaced ⅛ to ¼ inch (3 to 6mm) apart are also attractive.

When choosing depth of topstitching, remember that buttons when buttoned must not cover any of the topstitching.

Topstitching is almost always more professional when done from the outside of the garment. To topstitch lapels that turn back from a button and buttonhole, stitch from facing side until you reach the point they reverse. (This is the side that will be visible when the garment is worn.) Turn garment side up to complete topstitching. To conceal thread ends, knot end carefully and closely by hand. Thread a needle with it, and use needle to slip thread between facing and garment, emerging 1 inch (2.5cm) or more from knot. Clip thread. Press edges again after topstitching.

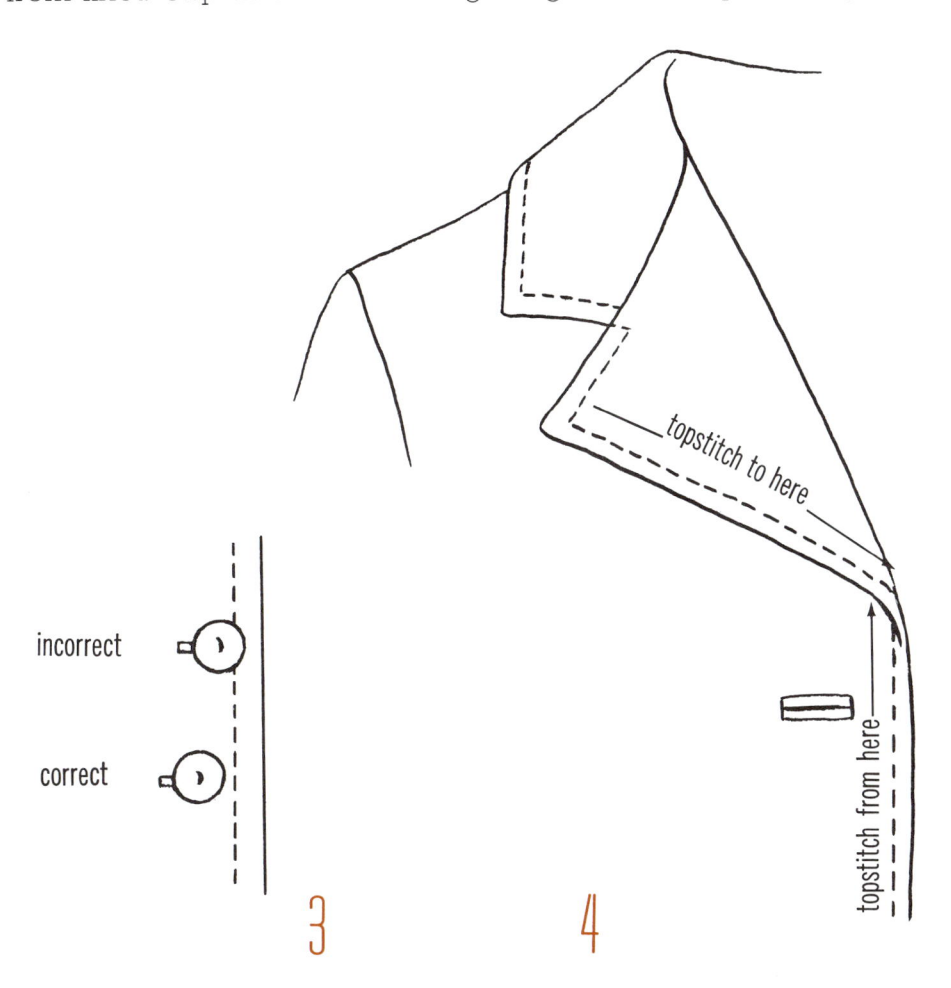

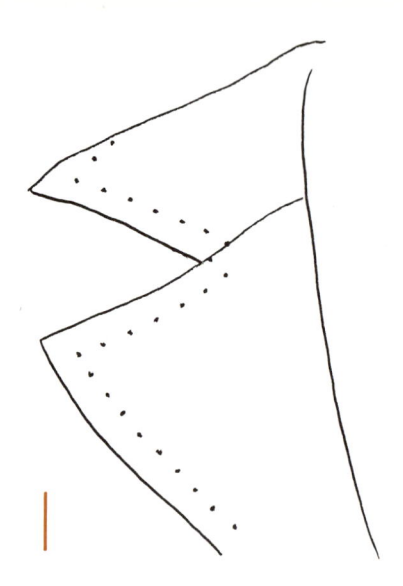

Hand picking is an edge finish frequently used on wool, flannel, cashmere, fleece, gabardine, and double knits in tailored, sporty garments. It is done ¼ to 1 inch (6mm to 2.5cm) from edges, depending upon fabric and style of garment. This stitch is done with double thread. You can use single buttonhole twist on garments that will be dry cleaned (buttonhole twist is not colorfast). After threading the needle, run the thread through beeswax, and press it with a warm iron to keep it from snarling. Press and pound edge to be stitched.

The stitch must go through the interfacing but need not penetrate the underside of the garment. On the topside of the garment leave approximately ¼ inch (6mm) between pick stitches. After stitching for several inches, wrap the thread in the needle around the finger and draw the thread firm to lie straight in the garment. Press and pound again after stitching.

PLEATS IN SLEEVES AND JACKET BACKS
Pleats in jacket backs and pleat openings in sleeves are finished the same way on the underside. Insert interfacing in the hem of sleeve or garment, pages 29, 42–43. Then stitch together two edges, including hem, at **a**. Press pleat in place, and attach edge **a** to hem as far up as top of hem. Insert lining in sleeve as if there were no pleat (page 49); the pleats in both sleeves and jacket back will be held in perfect alignment.

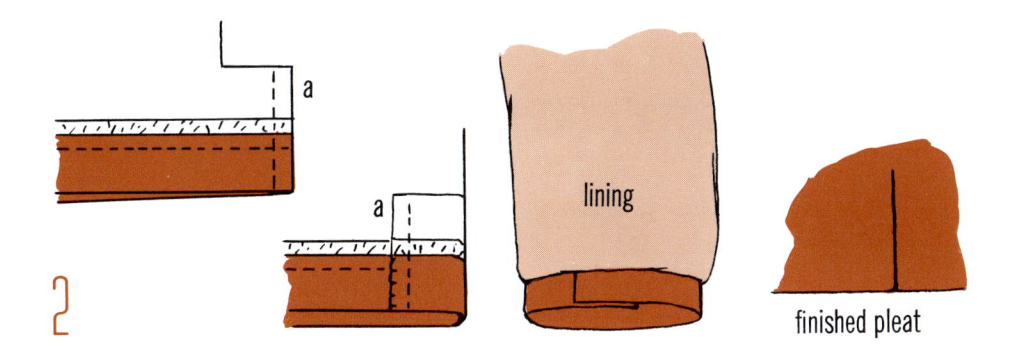

LABELS

A couturiere touch is to make your own labels from a piece of satin or grosgrain ribbon or a piece of matching lining. In your own handwriting write or print your initials, first name, or nickname. Embroider it using embroidery floss and your favorite embroidery stitch. Catchstitch or slipstitch to finished garment at center back neckline or inside front facing. Turning ends back diagonally adds a nice touch.

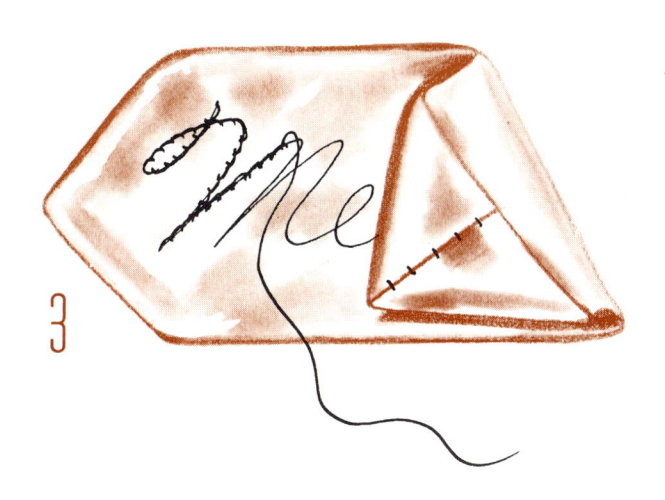

WAISTBANDS

The following are two excellent techniques for making waistbands in heavy fabrics.

To make a waistband that will finish 1¼ inches wide (3.2cm) use a lengthwise strip 3⅛ inches (7.8cm) wide and about 4 inches (10cm) longer than the waist measurement. Cut or tear using selvage **a** as one edge. With a crosswise-ribbed fabric such as bengaline use a crosswise-grain strip for the band. You will also need a lengthwise strip of interfacing 2 inches (5cm) wide. If you are using press-on interfacing, see page 62.

Place interfacing ¼ inch (6mm) from edge, **b**, of band. Stitch interfacing to band at **c**. Press band, rolling in place from edge **a** toward edge **b**; bring edge **a** to ⅝ inch (1.5cm) from edge **b** when pressing. Stitch interfacing along edge **b**, but do not open band flat again to do so; begin and end stitching 1 inch (2.5cm) from each end. Pressing usually brings interfacing edge to meet edge **b**. Try band on waist, holding with firmness preferred, to determine the size of waistband.

To attach waistband to skirt place edge **b** on waist edge of skirt, right sides of band and skirt together, as shown. Band overlap extends 1 inch (2.5cm) beyond front placket. There should be 2 or more inches (5 or more cm) for underlap on back of placket.

If skirt is stitched together for a fitting, the zipper is not inserted, but band is baste-stitched to skirt. If fit is satisfactory, loosen band from skirt at each side of placket in order to insert zipper before finishing the band.

With skirt side up, sew band to the skirt on seamline; press seam up, and trim band seam allowance to ¼ inch (6mm). To finish ends of band, fold right sides together. Interfacing at edge **b** was not stitched all the way out to ends to make this possible. Selvage edge, **a**, should meet seamline. The underlap end, **b**, is stitched to a point beginning at end of placket. Trim seams on both ends to ¼ inch (6mm), and round off corners. Turn ends right side out and press. Turn band right side out; selvage will fall in place to seamline; pin. With a long whipstitch, catch selvage of band to seamline of skirt.

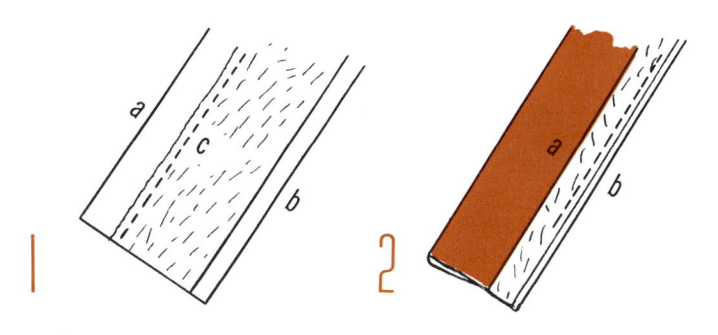

If band could not possibly be cut with one edge on the selvage, then the raw edge can be staystitched and finished with pinking or zigzag stitching, or it can be staystitched and bound with seam tape. Follow instructions for attaching selvage edge to skirt. For heavy fabrics this eliminates a seam at the inside edge of the band. Topstitch all around waistband, if desired.

The band may be finished with a button and buttonhole. Two hooks and eyes will support the underlap. A third hook and eye can be used at the front edge instead of the button and buttonhole. Final press the band.

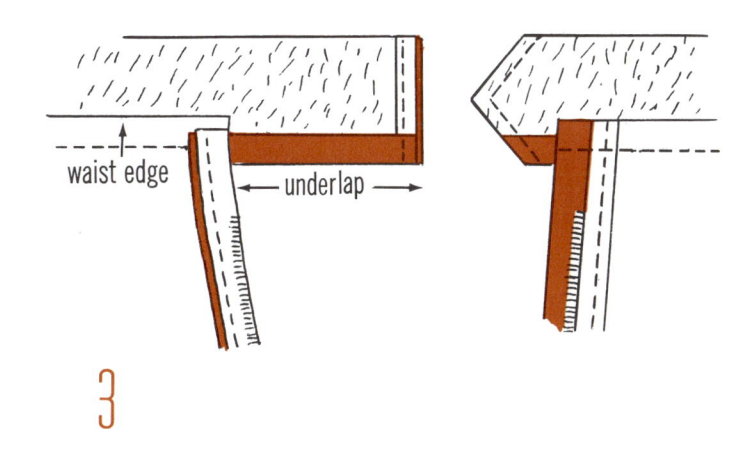

BELTING GROSGRAIN FOR THE BACK OF A BAND

Grosgrain used on the back of the band makes a flatter, closer-fitting band for a skirt from heavy fabric. Buy grosgrain in the width desired for the finished band. Tear or cut a strip of fabric on lengthwise grain, the width of grosgrain plus two seam allowances and 3 or 4 inches (7.5 or 10cm) longer than the waist. With a crosswise-ribbed fabric like bengaline, use a crosswise-grained strip. Lap grosgrain ⅝ inch (1.5cm) on one edge of strip for band, and stitch along edge of grosgrain. Press grosgrain in place on back of band. Stitch to skirt as in preceding method, but eliminate the point on the front edge.

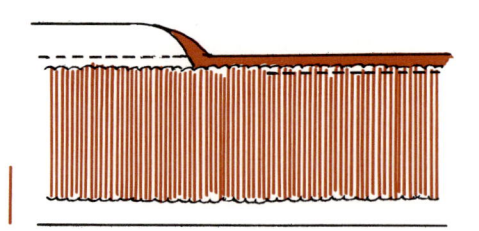

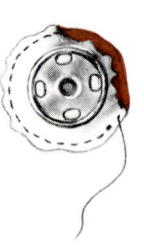

CLOSURES

SILK SNAPS

It is a couturiere touch to cover snaps with the matching print of dress or blouse, or from lining fabric.

Use snap size number two or three. Cut a circle the size of a small spool of thread from lining or other fabric. Punch a hole with a stiletto, and place lining over snap. Stitch around edge of lining; draw up thread and fasten neatly on underside of snap.

Place second circle over second half of snap. Close the snap, and while the snap is together, stitch around edge of second lining; draw up thread and fasten neatly on underside of snap. If fabric has a tendency to ravel, apply clear nail polish to raw edges.

When sewing to garment feel for holes in snaps with the needle. Be certain to sew snap to garment through holes of snap.

The projection should be sewn to the under side of overlap and the socket to top side of underlap.

SUNKEN SNAPS

Instead of being covered with lining fabric, the snap top (ball) may be placed under facing of garment, through which the snap head protrudes. This is known as a sunken snap. It has the advantage of being inconspicuous when the facing is turned back. When hand sewing the top half of snap to facing, do not stitch through interfacing or underlining, except on very light fabrics. The socket half of snap is covered as for a silk snap and stitched to garment in normal way.

BUTTONS

The kind of thread used to attach a button to a garment is determined by the weight of the fabric. Regular mercerized (size 50), nylon, or polyester thread will do the job on most mediumweight fabrics. Buttonhole twist — silk that has been twisted into a strong, lustrous thread — is heavier. It is used in a single strand and is especially useful where strength without bulk is desired for closures that will have heavy wear. To attach buttons to heavy garments — overcoats, raincoats, and jackets — run thread through beeswax; press with warm iron.

Buttons are placed on the garment after all other construction has been finished. To mark for buttons on garments that open from top to bottom, as on jackets, coats, and vests, lay garment so that the outsides of the two closure edges align exactly. (Insides of facings will be together.) If necessary, use a few pins to hold in place. Then place a pin through the front of the buttonhole at the center line. This marks the correct place to attach the button.

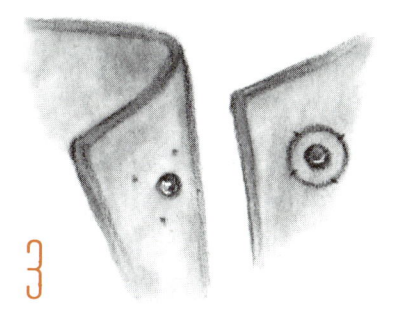

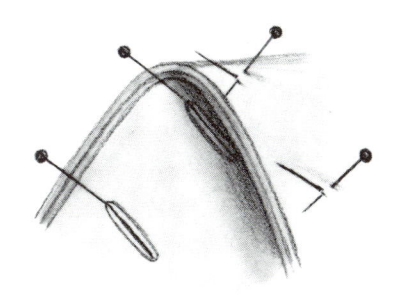

83

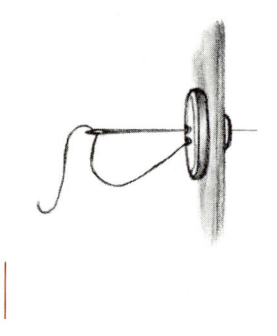

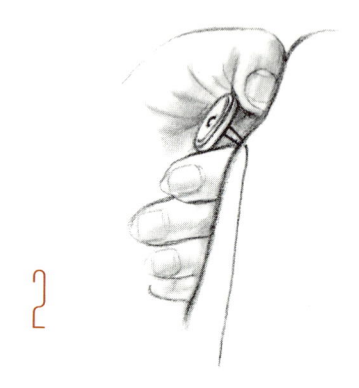

If you are working with a placket-type closure that is open at only one end, lay garment on flat surface, and lap buttonhole side of closure over button area. Match any markings for center front (or back). Place pin through front of buttonhole at center front. This marks button location.

Buttons need a firm backing. Avoid sewing a button on a single thickness of fabric. If button area is to receive a lot of wear and strain, it must be reinforced. Reinforce light- or mediumweight fabrics by using a small piece of fabric under the button area. Fabric piece may be attached to the button area on the inside of the garment with fusible web, or an iron-on fabric may be used. Reinforce buttons on heavy fabric with a small stay button on the inside of the garment. As you attach outer button to garment, sew through the stay button, too.

A shank is always necessary when a buttonhole lies between the button and the garment and the button is to be used as a closure. It is not necessary when a button serves only a decorative purpose. Some shanks are built into the button, but with sew-through buttons and buttons with a fabric shank, the shank must be made of thread as the button is attached to the garment.

Use a double strand of thread with a secure knot at one end. (If you are using buttonhole twist, use only a single strand to avoid tangling.) If your needle has a large enough eye, you may use two double strands to make four for sewing; you will need to take only half as many stitches. Knotting the strands separately helps to keep them from twisting.

Conceal thread knot as you begin by slipping needle under button. Bring thread into fabric, and take a small stitch to secure thread and knot in fabric.

With the thumb on top and forefinger under the button and the other fingers under the fabric, sew through button and fabric the necessary number of times to hold the button securely. The forefinger holds the button up from the fabric to make a shank the required length for the thickness of the buttonhole.

Bring needle and thread between button and garment, and wind thread several times around the shank threads. Run needle and thread through shank a few times; then draw needle and thread to inside of garment to finish. Finish by securing thread with several backstitches. Cut off remaining thread.

Shank buttons may require additional shanks if extra give is needed or if buttons have only fabric shank. Follow instructions for sew-through buttons. Follow same instructions for finishing off as for sew-through buttons.

With a heavy button that keeps wearing away the thread that holds it, sew it to the long eye of a hook and eye. With it, the thread won't wear away.

85

BUTTONHOLE SIZE

To determine the size of buttonhole, pin a strip of paper or seam binding around the largest part of the button. Remove button; without unpinning strip, measure from pin to fold to determine correct size of buttonhole.

BUTTONHOLES

The following is a popular way to make buttonholes. Begin by marking buttonhole locations vertically and horizontally. Machine-baste crosswise lines on interfacing through to the outside of garment. Then baste the center front line the length of all the buttonholes. Determine the finished buttonhole length, and baste a second line this distance from, and parallel to, the center front line. On delicate fabrics that will retain stitch marks of machine basting, use hand basting.

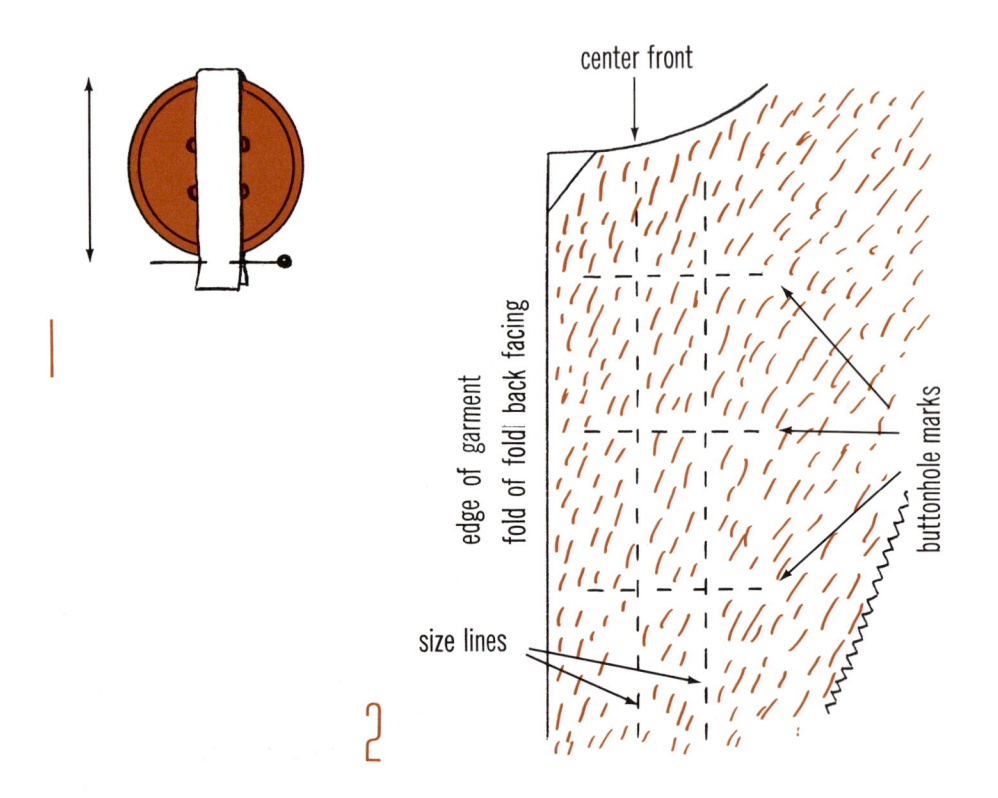

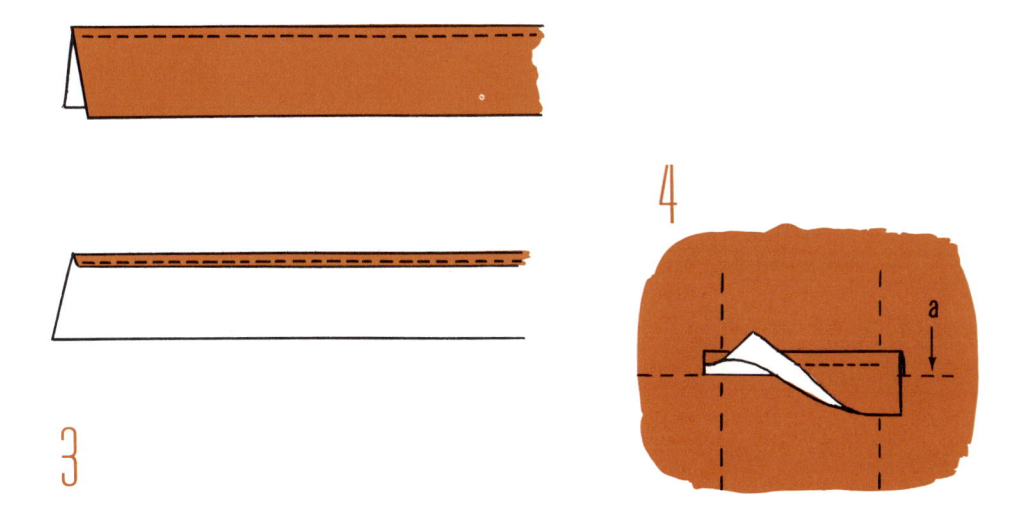

Buttonhole length should be at least the diameter of the button plus its thickness. Usually, tailored buttonholes are not made shorter than 1 inch (2.5cm). In a heavy coat, buttonholes should be 1¼ to 1½ inches (3.2–3.8cm) long even if the button requires less.

To prepare a finishing strip, tear or cut on lengthwise grain a strip of fabric about 1½ inches (3.8cm) wide. Make an extra long strip, and cut it as needed. Each strip should be 1 inch (2.5cm) longer than the buttonhole will be. For checks, plaids, stripes, and ribbed fabrics, use true bias strips. These will make contrasting, decorative buttonholes. With wrong sides together, fold finishing strip in half, and press to crease. Stitch a tuck ⅛ inch (3mm) wide on folded edge of strip. It may help you to use thread of a slightly different color for this stitching. The presser foot can serve as a guide for straight stitching. Trim down one of the raw edges to exact width of tuck.

Place this short raw edge on guideline **a** on outside of garment with finishing strip extending ½ (1.3cm) inch beyond one size line. The deep raw edge will then lie over the narrow one. Stitch from one size line to the other through line of tuck-stitching. Use a short machine stitch, and lockstitch at beginning and end. (If it is difficult to lockstitch precisely at size lines, leave threads and pull them to underside to tie by hand.) The tuck stitching does not show in illustrations. It will be under this stitching line.

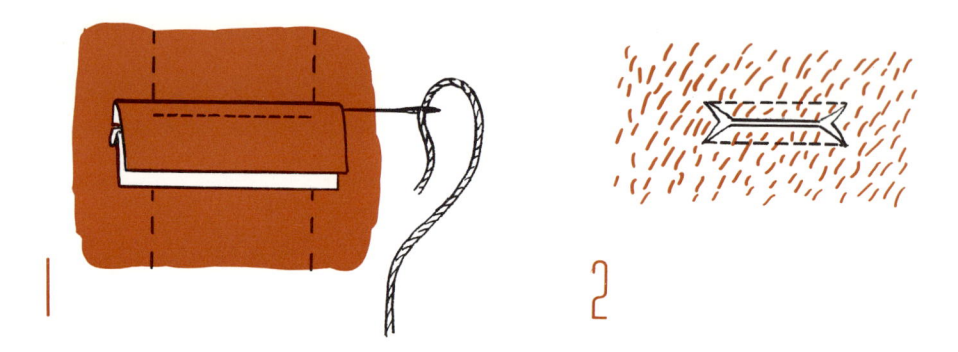

Cut off strip at end, ½ inch (1.3cm) beyond stitching line. Sew on second strip. Repeat for each buttonhole. If buttonhole is made of a bias strip or of lightweight fabric, such as silk or linen, insert yarn or thin cord through both tucks on finishing strips, using needlepoint needle.

Remove all buttonhole basting from garment. On inside of garment starting at center of buttonhole, make clip through interfacing and fabric, and cut diagonally to corners, leaving triangles ¼ to ⅜ inch (6mm to 1.2cm) long at ends of buttonhole. While cutting, hold the strips out of way of shears by placing finger under them on right side of garment.

Turn finishing strips to inside. Do not handle triangles. Carefully pull ends of strips to square the corners of buttonhole. The folded edges now meet in corners of the buttonhole.

Place garment right side up on sewing machine. Turn back edge of garment to reveal triangle and end of strips. Stitch triangle to strips, going back and forth many times to fasten securely from knots at base of triangle all the way to end of strip. This connecting line squares the corners. Stitch opposite end of buttonhole the same way. Press buttonhole in direction of strip.

After front facing is stitched on and pressed in place, the buttonholes will be finished through the facing. Place a pin through each end of the buttonhole to determine where the facing is to be slashed under buttonhole. You may mark a location point through buttonholes with tracing paper and tracing wheel if it is easier.

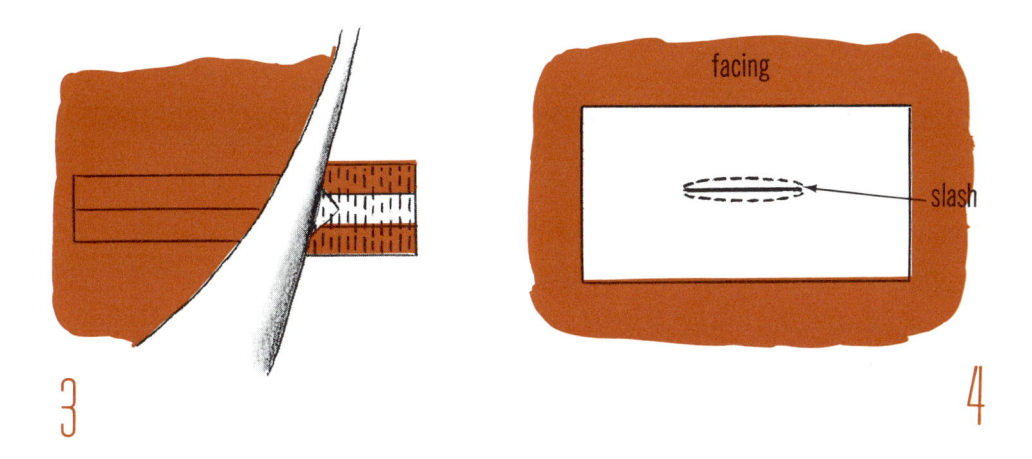

Next, stitch a bias strip of organdy or other fine, firm fabric over slash line on right side of facing, using shortest machine stitches. Stitch a few threads from slash line on each side of it.

Slash facing and organdy on slash line. Turn organdy to inside of facing, and press. Trim away all but ½ inch (1.3cm) around opening.

Whipstitch finished edge on facing side to back of buttonhole. Use a single thread run through beeswax holder. This method is easier, and the buttonhole is more durable than if you cut and turn in raw edges of facing. This step should not be done until you have completed any other required handwork on facings.

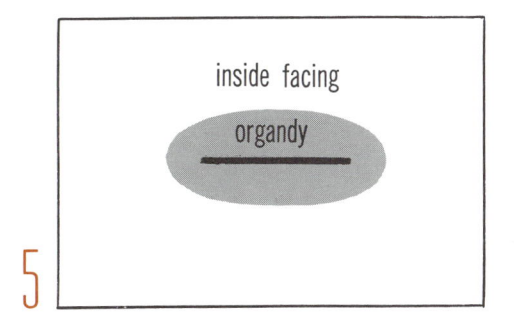

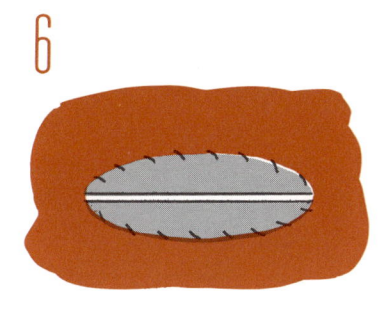

CHANGING POINTS TO CURVES
If you have a bulky, wiry, or other problem fabric that is difficult to turn into beautiful points at corners of collars, lapels, pocket flaps, or belt ends, simply cut them into an oval or round instead of a point. When sewing it is wise to let your fabric tell you what to do.

HOLDING FRONT FACINGS IN LINE
With spongy or heavy fabrics and those that do not hold their press very well, some hand tacking will serve to hold the facings in line. About 1 inch (2.5cm) or more apart, and with loose hand stitches, tack the facing to the interfacing or underlining. Two rows should be adequate for the facing width. Use one row in the middle of the back neck facing.

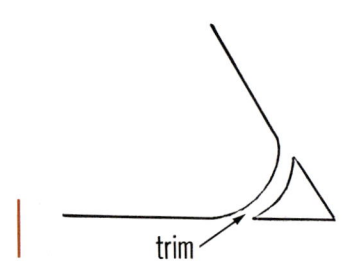

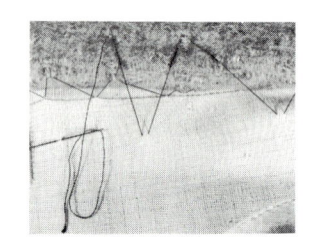

INTERLINING A COAT
If underlining and a lining are used, a coat may be warm enough without an interlining, but if you want one, there are many choices on the market. Take interlining into consideration when fitting your garment because most will add some bulk.

Durable satins that are backed with wool, metallic reflective finish, or laminated foam insulation are available. These are cut, stitched together, and inserted in the coat like regular lining with the following differences:
  1. The coat and the interlining are hemmed separately.
  2. The edges of facings are handled exactly as in the technique for separate interlining that follows.

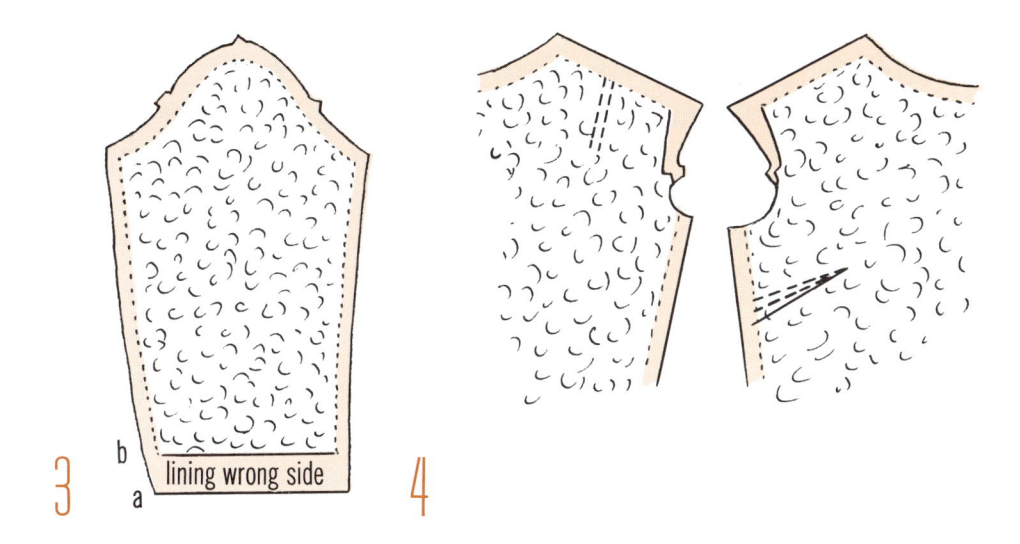

Separate interlinings can be used with regular linings. Lamb's wool is a popular choice, or there is a very lightweight polyester nonwoven fleece available.

Instead of buying interlining, you can cut up old, lightweight woolen blankets or garments, which are equally satisfactory.

After the regular lining has been cut out, the separate interlining is cut like the lining except for the following differences:
1. The sleeve lining is cut to the finished length of the coat sleeve, **a**, plus an extra ½ inch (1.3cm). The interlining is cut only to the top of the coat sleeve hem, **b**.
2. The coat lining is cut to the finished length of the coat plus 1 inch (2.5cm) for ease. The interlining is cut only to the top of the coat hem. However, it may be cut to extend as far as over the hips; it need not extend all the way to the lower edge of the coat. This eliminates some bulk and weight.

Do not cut a center back pleat in the interlining, even if the lining has one. Do not cut on extra fabric at armholes of the interlining as you did for the lining. Darts in interlining are stitched separately and then stitched again ¼ inch (6mm) from the first row of stitching so that they will lie flat.

91

Staystitch interlining to lining on seamline at all edges except armholes above notches and lower edges of sleeves. Stitch seams on seamline, press open, and trim away interfacing to seamline. Trim away interlining up to staystitching on all other staystitched edges—sleeve cap, front facing edges, shoulders, back neckline, and below notches at armholes. See art number 4, page 91.

Edges of coat facings would be bulky if lining and interlining were stitched in one seam to coat facing. The following technique is used to obtain a flat, professional edge on a facing. Stitch a continuous bias strip of lining fabric 1½ inches (3.8cm) wide exactly on seamline around front and back neck facings, beginning and ending at hem edge of coat, as shown. (Right sides of facing and strip are together.)

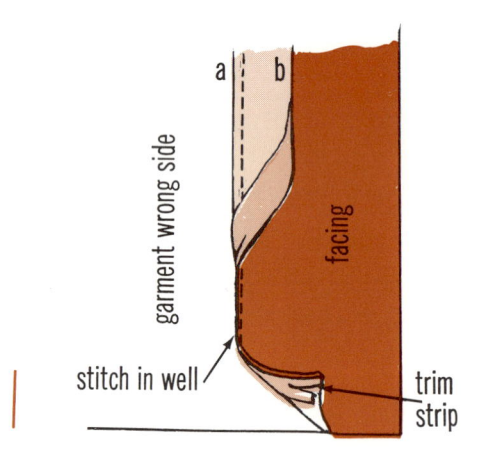

Trim seam allowance, **a**, to ¼ inch (6mm); turn bias to underside of facings without turning in raw edge, **b**; press in place. Stitch in well of seamline at machine or with a running stitch by hand to hold bias in place; trim away excess width of bias. If lining is bulky, use lightweight fabric for bias strip.

The lining and interlining are inserted in a coat exactly as in a jacket, page 50, with one exception: The bound seamline of the facings is pinned over the lining to keep exactly to the staystitching line. Slipstitch lining to facings through machine stitching on facings and staystitching on lining.

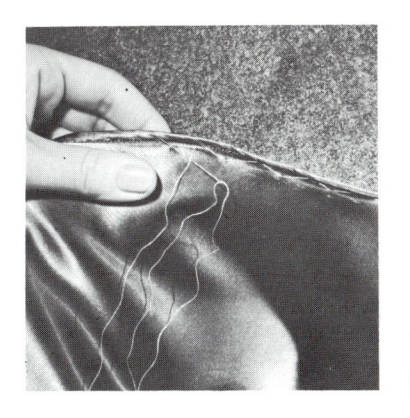

For some styles of coats, if you prefer to keep the lining free at the hem, place a piece of lining over underlining for 8 to 10 inches (20.5 to 25.5cm) above hemline. Catch this lining to the coat at each seamline with a chainstitch 1 inch (2.5cm) long. Hemline of coat should be finished with a piece of bias, as for facings, preceding paragraph.

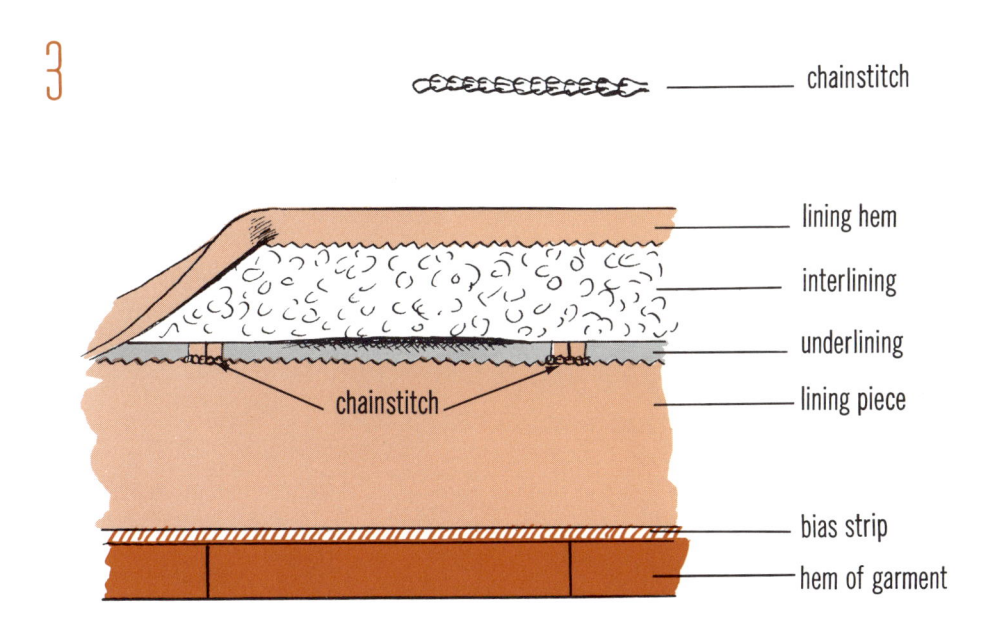

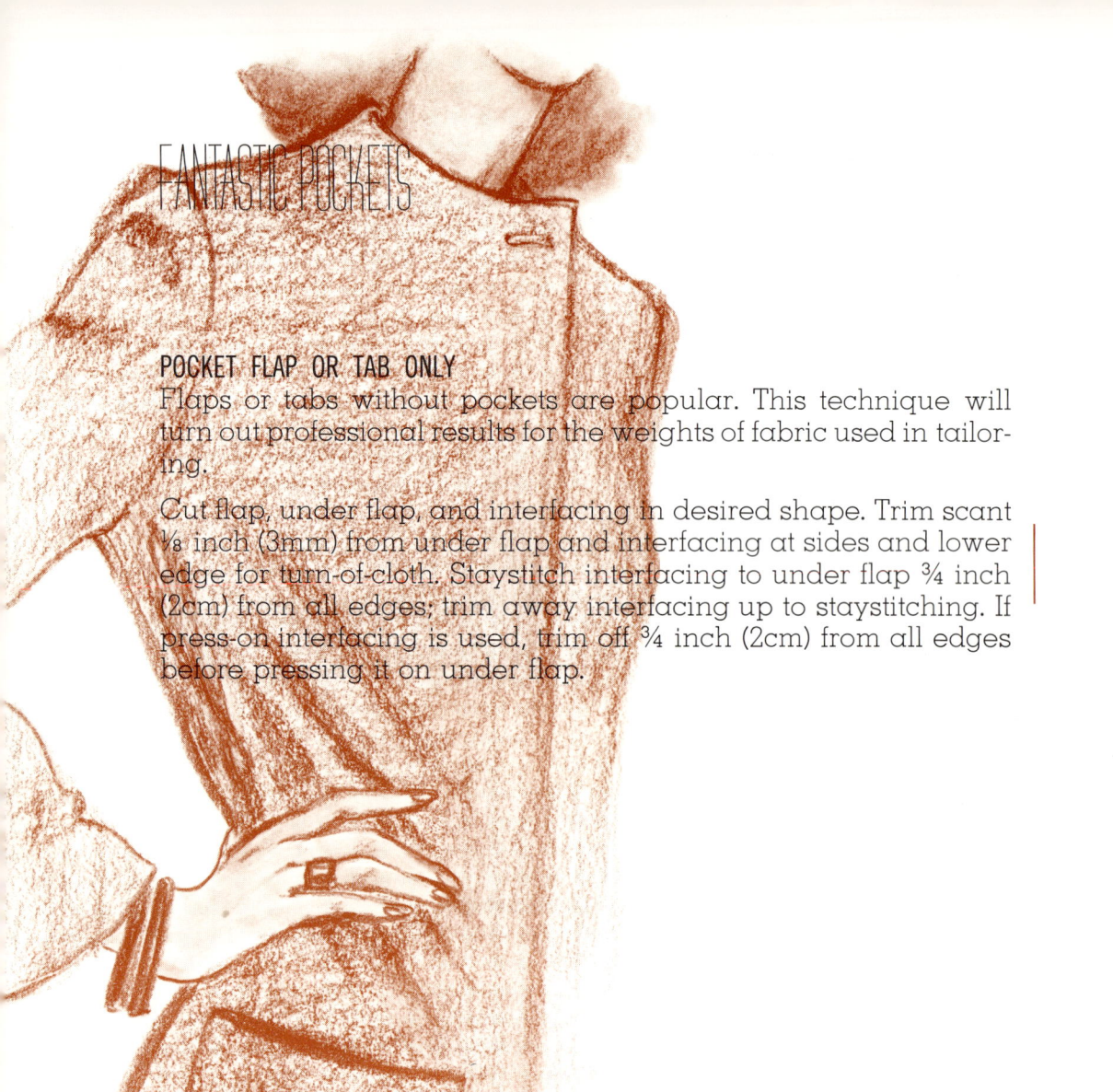

FANTASTIC POCKETS

POCKET FLAP OR TAB ONLY

Flaps or tabs without pockets are popular. This technique will turn out professional results for the weights of fabric used in tailoring.

Cut flap, under flap, and interfacing in desired shape. Trim scant ⅛ inch (3mm) from under flap and interfacing at sides and lower edge for turn-of-cloth. Staystitch interfacing to under flap ¾ inch (2cm) from all edges; trim away interfacing up to staystitching. If press-on interfacing is used, trim off ¾ inch (2cm) from all edges before pressing it on under flap.

Right sides together, join top flap to under flap at sides and lower edge. Press one seam allowance back, and stagger seam allowances. Trim corners, turn, and press.

Roll flap on your fingers at the top to allow for turn-of-cloth when seam allowance is turned under; stitch raw edges together just outside seamline.

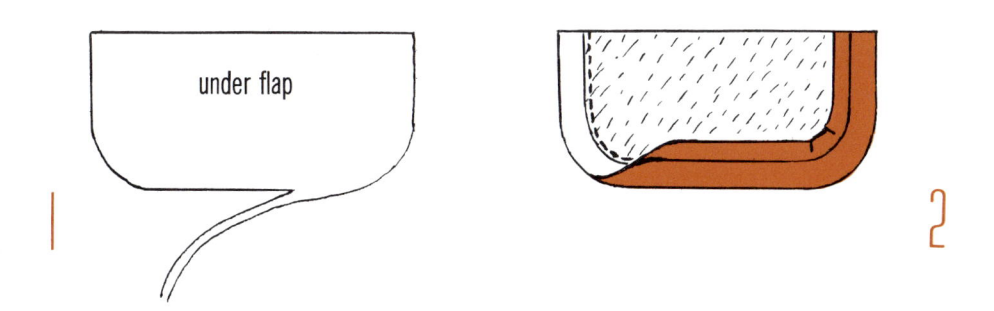

Place flap upside down on garment right side, and stitch on seamline. Stitch again ⅛ to ¼ inch (3 to 6mm) below seamline.

Trim seam allowance close to stitching. Turn flap down and press. If desired, topstitch upper edge close to edge or ¼ inch (6mm) from it.

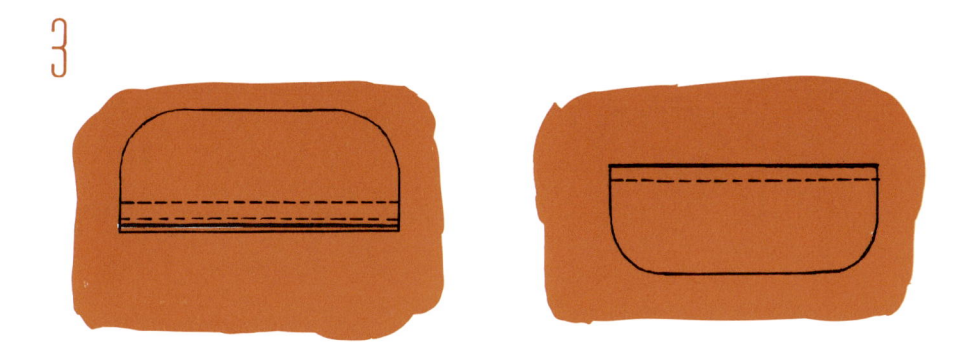

FANTASTIC PATCH POCKET I

Cut pocket and lining according to pattern tissue. The pocket preferably should have a foldback hem. Interface pocket to fold of hem, if required, and staystitch pocket ⅝ inch (1.5cm) from edge. Stitch lining to pocket, and press open seam.

Press the pocket into its finished shape. A piece of cardboard cut to finished size of pocket will help in pressing around curves.

Mark pocket lining ¾ inch (2cm) from edges. Pin pocket lining to garment in correct position, and stitch lining and pocket to garment to the depth of the pocket hem, ¾ inch (2cm) from edge, as shown. Be certain to make a good knot at both upper edges of pocket hem. Press seam allowances toward inside of pocket, and trim if desired.

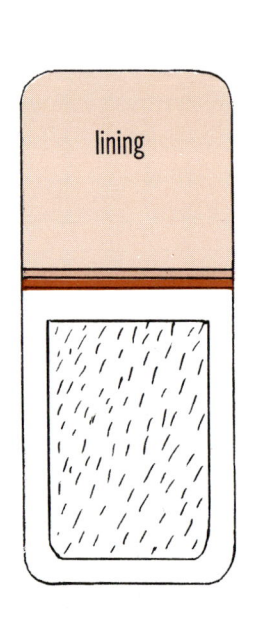

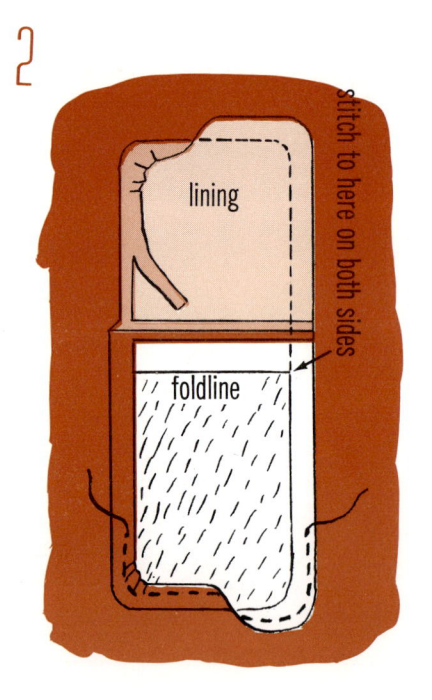

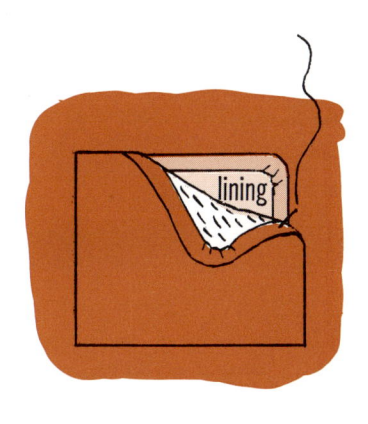

Fold pocket on top of pocket lining, and pin in place. The raw edges will be enclosed. With invisible hand stitches from underneath, sew pocket into position. Press lightly. The ¾-inch (2-cm) seam on lining takes care of the turn-of-the-cloth. The seam can be made even deeper on heavy fabric.

PATCH POCKET II

This pocket is frequently used on blazer jackets, suits, sport coats, and men's sport jackets. It can be applied with the following method only when the lower edges are curved. This pocket cannot be interfaced, and there is no way to allow for the turn-of-the-cloth.

The outside pocket piece is cut 1 inch (2.5cm) deeper than the lining because it turns back to make a 1-inch (2.5-cm) hem at the top of the pocket. With right sides together, stitch pocket piece and lining together on top edges with ¼-inch (6-mm) seam allowances. Press seam open, turn pocket right side out, and press 1-inch (2.5-cm) hem at top.

fabric	fabric wrong side
underlining	
interfacing either side	interfacing either side
interlining either side	
lining	lining wrong side

Stitch together pocket piece and lining precisely ¼ inch (6mm) from raw edges. Fold in half and snip pocket at exact center on lower edge, **a**. Notches should be clipped from seam allowance at **b** and **b** — the deepest part of curve.

On the right side of the garment, place the pocket in position on the location lines. Mark with chalk or hand-baste a line on garment exactly around raw edges of pocket; **b** and **b** are at top of pocket. Mark the center line, **c**, of pocket on garment. Remove pocket and mark a second line ½ inch (1.3cm) inside first line. This is the guideline for sewing on pocket.

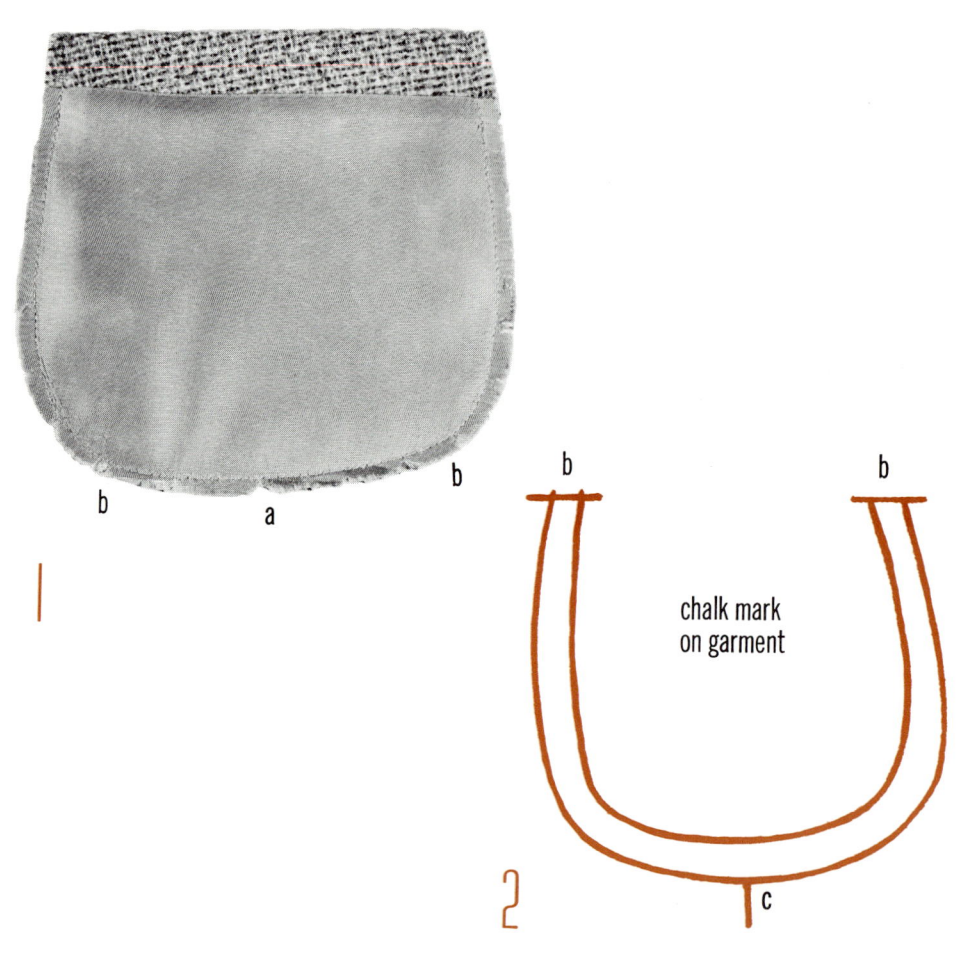

chalk mark on garment

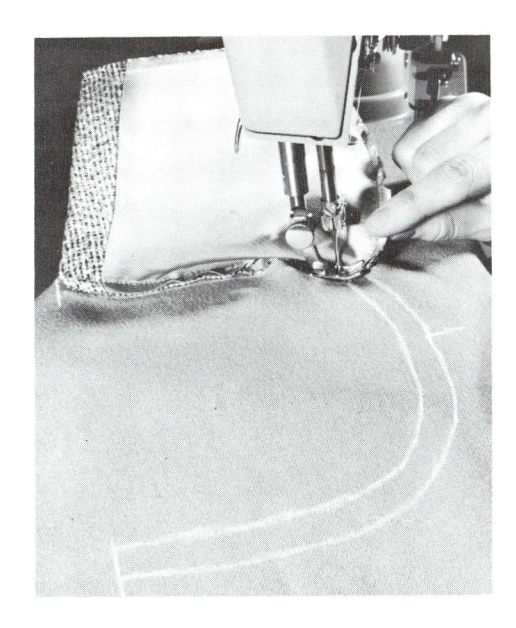

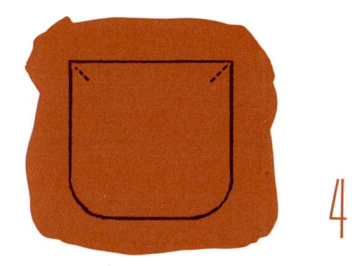

Match raw edges of pocket to right side down inner marking line. Stitch pocket to garment through first stitching, exactly ¼ inch (6mm) from edge. Be sure the center of the pocket keys to center marking, **c**, on the garment. The pocket begins to close in on the presser foot, but the raw edge still can be keyed easily to the inner marking line to complete stitching around the pocket.

Press flat. Trim ¼ inch (6mm) diagonally from upper corners inside pocket. Bar-tack each side at upper edge by stitching back and forth at machine several times for reinforcement, or slipstitch by hand for ¼ inch (6mm) across upper edge.

WELT POCKET

For heavy fabrics it is essential to use the regulation welt pocket method that follows. The Modified Welt Pocket, pages 104–106, is preferable for tailoring lightweight fabrics. The regulation welt pocket should be 4 inches (10cm) long when used above the waistline; below the waistline it should be 4 to 6 inches (10 to 15cm) long.

Baste location line, **a**, and size lines, **b**, through to outside of fabric. The area under the pocket must be interfaced to reinforce the opening and preserve the pocket line. Use a lengthwise strip of muslin or a strip of press-on interfacing.

For pocket location on lengthwise or crosswise grain make the strip 2 inches (5cm) deep and 2 inches longer than the pocket opening. For a diagonal pocket location make the strip deep enough to extend 1 inch (2.5cm) on each side of location line and 2

inches longer than pocket opening. Place interfacing on underside of garment to cover location and size lines. Pin muslin or press interfacing in place.

To make welt, cut on lengthwise grain a strip of fabric 1½ inches (3.8cm) deep and 2 inches (5cm) longer than the finished pocket will be. Fold welt lengthwise, wrong sides together. Press; stitch ¼ inch (6mm) from edge.

Cut upper pocket piece from lining fabric on crosswise grain. Cut same width as welt and the depth desired for finished pocket plus seam allowances. Match raw edges of welt to top edge of upper pocket piece, right side up. Stitch welt and pocket piece together over first stitching on welt. With welt side down place upper edges of welt and pocket piece on location line on right side of garment; welt and pocket unit should lie below the location line and extend the width of a seam allowance on each side of size lines. Stitch between size lines through welt and pocket on previous stitching. Shorten stitches for first and last ½ inch (1.3cm) for reinforcement.

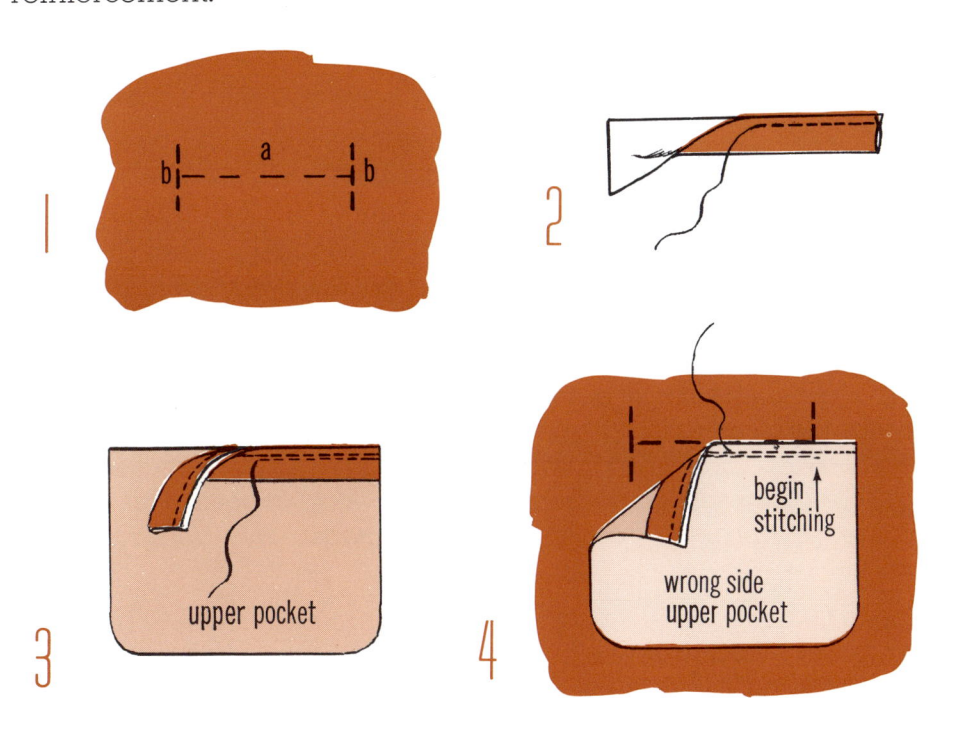

Place under pocket piece face down on right side of garment above location line. It should extend the width of a seam allowance beyond each size line. Grain of under pocket should match the grain of garment. Stitch pocket to garment between size lines ¼ inch (6cm) from raw edge, again using a short stitch for first and last ½ inch (1.3cm).

Stitch carefully, and check for accuracy. The width of the welt must be exactly the same as the distance between the two stitching lines. If the welt is ½ inch (1.3cm) deep, the stitching lines must be exactly ½ inch (1.3cm) apart so the welt will fit perfectly and lie flat. The stitching lines should not extend beyond the size lines.

Remove basting from garment at location and size lines. On inside of garment, slash between stitching lines, starting at center. Cut through interfacing and garment, and cut diagonally to corners, leaving triangles ½ inch (1.3cm) long at ends of pocket opening. Turn pocket sections to inside. Pull ends of welt with care to square the corners. Press under pocket seam open in heavy fabrics.

When the pocket is turned the welt automatically turns to fill the ½ inch (1.3cm) space. Press carefully after turning. Understitch both pocket pieces along the top edges.

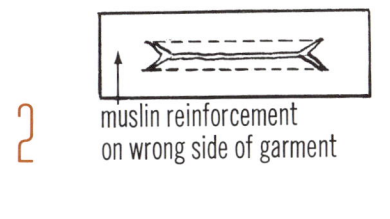

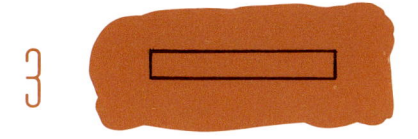

2 muslin reinforcement on wrong side of garment

3

Place garment right side up on sewing machine. Turn back garment to see triangle and pocket sections. Stitch triangle to pocket sections, stitching back and forth a number of times. This will fasten triangle from base to point securely to pocket. This stitching across base of triangle also squares end of pocket. Continue stitching around pocket sections to close pocket; round lower edges of pocket when stitching to keep lint from collecting. Repeat stitching at opposite triangle. Trim interfacing to ½ inch (1.3cm) around pocket opening.

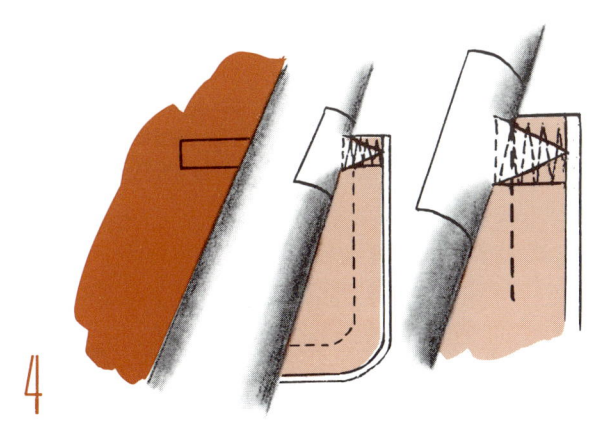

4

4

MODIFIED WELT POCKET

A pocket on the inside front lining of a coat is great for holding gloves or a scarf. It is also an excellent place to try out your pocket technique before attempting the pocket in your garment.

This pocket is used when tailoring lightweight fabrics. It is particularly useful for making silk and linen suits. (For medium- and heavyweight fabrics use Welt Pocket.) Make this ½ inch (1.3cm) deep and 3 to 6 inches (7.5 to 15cm) wide, depending upon its position. The higher the pocket placement, the shorter its length. When used below the waistline of a coat, the modified welt pocket should be 6 inches (15cm) long. It is generally better to place this pocket horizontally or vertically rather than at an angle.

Baste location line, **a**, and size lines, **b**, through to outside of fabric. The garment must be reinforced around the pocket opening. Use a lengthwise strip of muslin or press-on interfacing 2 inches (5cm) wide and 2 inches (5cm) longer than the opening. Place on underside of garment to cover location and size lines. Pin in place.

Use the lengthwise grain of fabric for the width of the pocket and the crosswise grain for the pocket depth. Cut or tear a strip of fabric 1 inch (2.5cm) wider than pocket opening and 1 inch (2.5cm)

basting — — — — — — — — — — — — — — — —

permanent stitching — — — — — — — — — — — —

longer than desired depth of pocket. This strip makes the welt and upper pocket piece. For the back pocket use fabric on same grain as garment, 1 inch (2.5cm) wider than the pocket opening and the desired depth of the pocket in length.

On fabric strip, for welt and upper pocket piece fold ¾ inch (2cm) on one lengthwise edge to wrong side, and press. Stitch ½ inch (1.3cm) from fold to form welt.

Place raw edge of welt on location marking line with each end extending ½ inch (1.3cm) beyond size lines, and wrong side of pocket section to right side of garment. Stitch on right side of welt between size lines over the stitching that formed the welt.

Place one horizontal edge of the strip for under pocket on location line. The raw edge should meet the raw edge of the welt, right side of pocket to right side of garment. Stitch ¼ inch (6mm) from raw edge between size lines. Check on the wrong side of garment for accuracy of stitching. The stitching lines should be ½ inch (1.3cm) apart. They should not extend beyond the size lines.

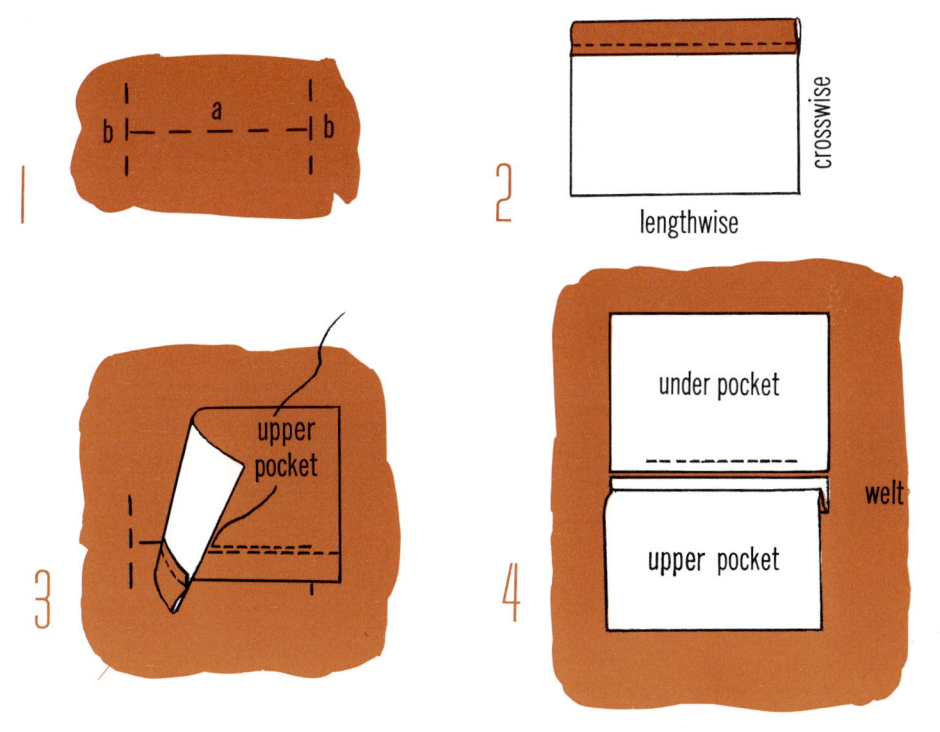

105

1

muslin reinforcement on wrong side of garment

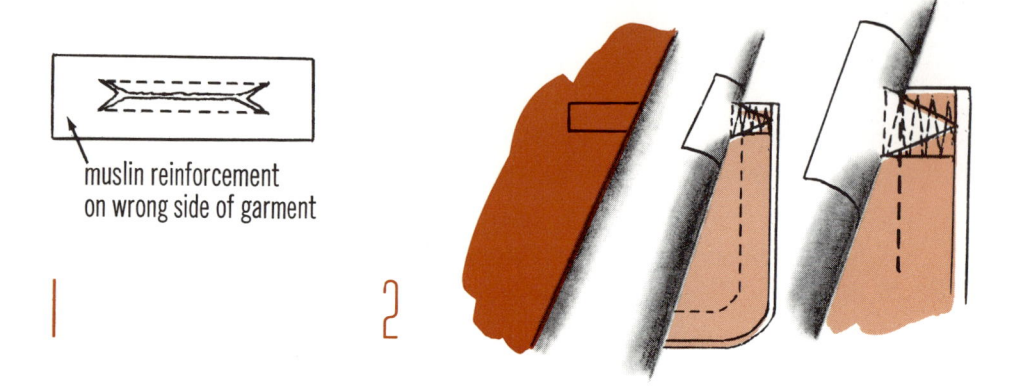

2

Remove location- and size-line basting stitches from garment. On wrong side of garment slash between stitching lines, starting at center. Cut through interfacing and garment. Cut diagonally to corners, leaving triangles ½ inch (1.3cm) long at ends of pocket opening. Turn pocket sections to inside. In lightweight fabrics press under-pocket seam down. Welt will fit opening perfectly.

Place garment right side up on sewing machine. Turn back garment so you can see triangle and pocket sections. Stitch triangle to pocket sections, stitching back and forth many times to securely join triangle from base to point to pocket. This stitching at base of triangle also squares ends of pocket. Continue stitching around pocket sections to close pocket, and repeat stitching at opposite triangle. When stitching, round lower edges of pocket to keep out lint. Trim interfacing to ½ inch (1.3cm) all around pocket opening.

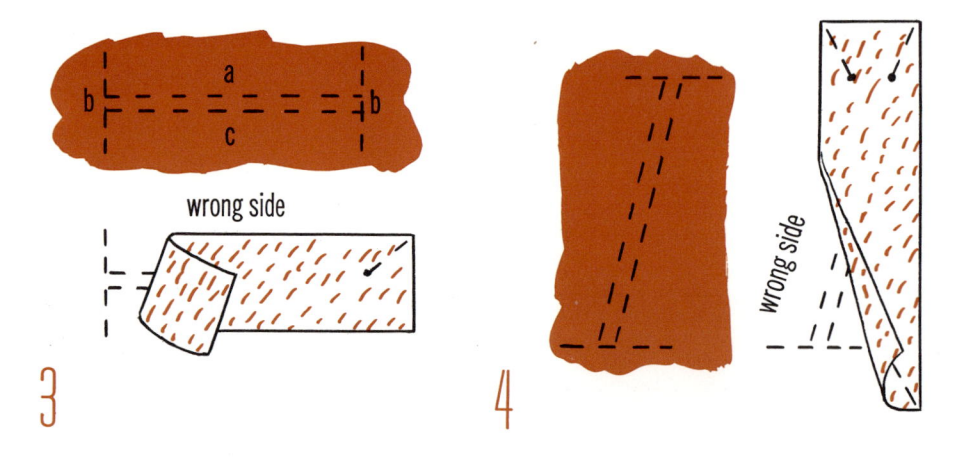

3

wrong side

4

wrong side

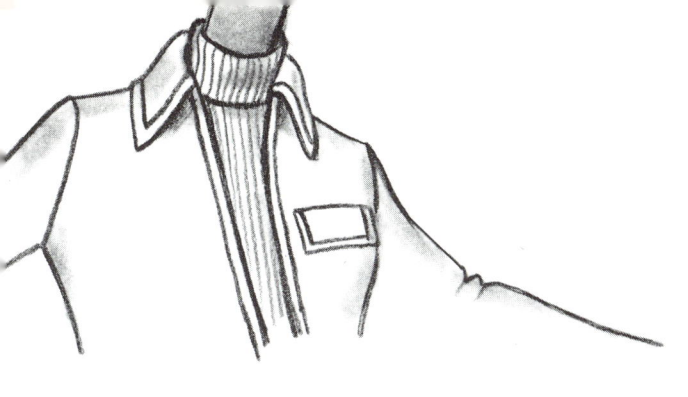

FLAP POCKET

A flap over a welt pocket is often used on tailored garments. Baste location line, **a**, and size lines, **b**, so they show on outside of garment. Baste a second crosswise line, **c**, ¼ inch (6mm) below location line **a**. The garment under the pocket must be interfaced to reinforce the opening and preserve the pocket line. Use a lengthwise strip of muslin or press-on interfacing. For pocket location on lengthwise or crosswise grain make the strip 2 inches (5cm) deep and 2 inches (5cm) longer than the pocket opening.

For a diagonal pocket location make the strip deep enough to extend 1 inch (2.5cm) on each side of location lines and 2 inches (5cm) longer than pocket opening. Place interfacing on underside of garment to cover location and size lines. Pin muslin or press interfacing in place.

The flap, the flap facing, and flap interfacing should be cut on same grain, 5¼ inches (13.1cm) by 3⅜ inches (8.5cm). Cut interfacing from corners of flap ¼ inch (6mm) beyond seamline to reduce bulk so flap will turn easily and lie in a perfect line. Staystitch regular interfacing, or use press-on and press, to flap facing ¾ inch (2cm) from edges **a** and **b** and ⅛ inch (3mm) from edge **c**. Trim interfacing close to stitching at edges **a** and **b**. With interfacing side up and right sides together, stitch flap to flap facing (under flap). Trim seam allowance edges to ⅛ inch (3mm) and ¼ inch (6mm) to stagger them—the wider edge should be on top.

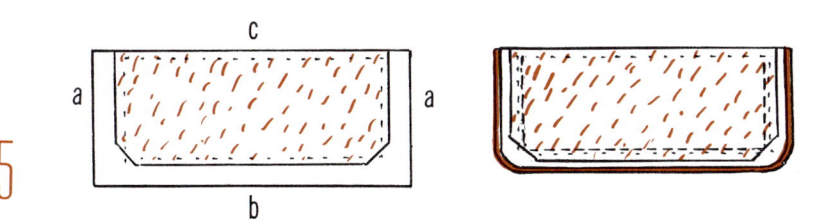

Round off corners to within a few threads of the stitching line. Turn right side out, press, and pound with block. Stitch raw edges of flap together ⅛ inch (3mm) from edge.

The under-pocket piece should be cut on same grain as garment. In heavy fabrics the lower three-fourths is cut from lining fabric to reduce bulk. This is seamed to the upper one-fourth of the pocket piece that is cut from garment fabric. Allow for this seam when cutting pocket piece. Raw edges of this seam lie outside of under pocket, next to garment when pocket is completed.

Match edge of flap to edge of under-pocket piece with ends of pocket extending the width of a seam allowance on each side. The underside of flap should face right side of pocket piece. Stitch together ⅛ inch (3cm) from raw edges, easing flap to pocket piece if pocket is to lie on hip or bustline curve of a fitted garment.

With flap side down on right side of garment, place under-pocket unit with top of flap ⅛ inch (3mm) beyond upper location line and between size lines. The stitching on pocket and flap should lie exactly on location line. Stitch pocket unit to garment on same line of stitching. Use short stitches for first and last ½ inch (1.3cm). Cut upper pocket piece on crosswise grain; this maintains shape of finished pocket opening. Place upper pocket piece on right side of garment. Top edge should extend ⅛ inch (3mm) above lower location line. Pocket piece should extend the width of a seam allowance on each side of size lines. Stitch between size lines ⅛ inch (3mm) from edge, again using short stitches for first and last ½ inch (1.3cm).

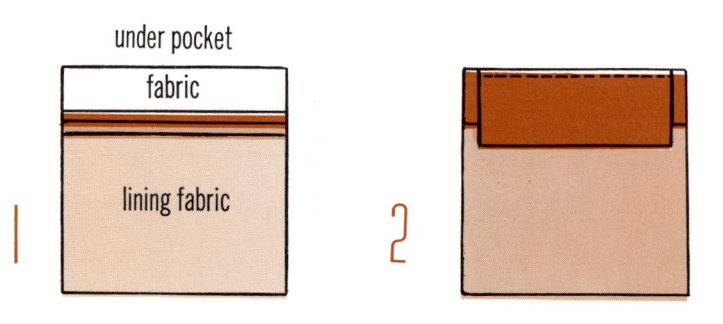

Stitching lines for upper and under pockets should be ¼ inch (6mm) apart. They should not extend beyond size lines. Check garment on wrong side for accuracy. Remove location and size-line basting. On wrong side of garment start at center between stitching lines and slash through interfacing and garment. Cut diagonally to corners leaving triangles ½ inch (1.3cm) long at ends of pocket opening. Turn pocket sections to wrong side. Pull ends of pocket pieces carefully to square the corners.

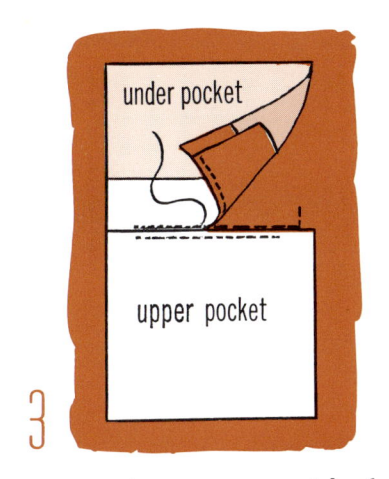

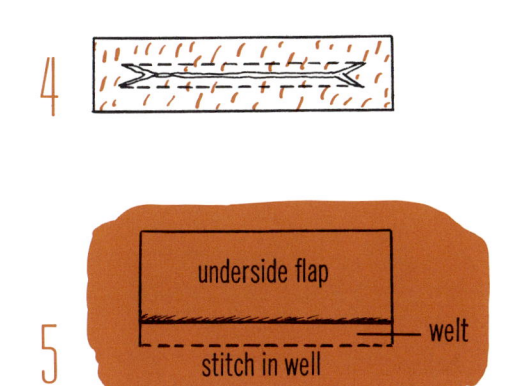

Fold top pocket piece up to form a narrow welt. (It will cover the seamline.) Press. Bevel a ⅛-inch (3-mm) seam allowance on bulky fabrics. With flap turned back, stitch in well of seamline to hold welt in place. Press flap so that it lies perfectly. Topstitch if desired.

Place garment right side up on sewing machine. Turn back garment to see triangles and pocket sections. Stitch triangle to pocket sections, stitching back and forth a number of times to fasten triangle from base to point securely to pocket. This stitching across base of triangle also squares end of pocket.

Continue stitching around pocket sections to close pocket; round lower edges of pocket when stitching to keep lint from collecting. Repeat stitching at opposite triangle. Trim interfacing to ½ inch (1.3cm) around pocket opening.

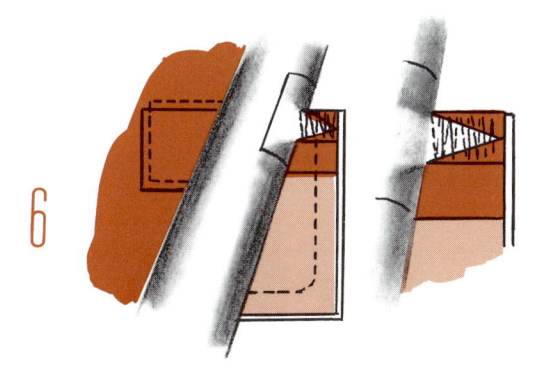

PRESSING

PRESSING ON GRAIN
As you know, the whole concept of grain perfection is essential to well-made clothes. The fabric must be grain-perfect. The pattern pieces must be cut and the seams stitched on grain. Grain is important in pressing as well. All seams must be pressed in the direction they were stitched. Pressing with grain will sometimes accomplish what stitching could not. If you do not press directionally, you will not be able to mold and shape your garment properly. Even when you are patting the garment lightly after steaming, you must respect the grain of the fabric.

MOISTURE
The correct amount of moisture is as important as the correct amount of heat. Too much moisture can damage the fabric or shrink it, while too little moisture will not mold the garment properly and will make it more difficult to flatten seams and edges.

Try a scrap of fabric to see how much moisture is required. Leave a portion of the scrap unpressed so you can see any change in the fabric more clearly. Certain fabrics, including some silks and nylons, press beautifully without moisture. Others, such as linen and "Qiana" nylon fabrics, require direct steam pressing.

Moisture in different strengths can be applied several ways: with the steam setting on the iron; with a dampened (never wet) cheesecloth or drill cloth; with spray or steam spray (not available on every iron).

To dampen a cheesecloth moisten about a third of the cloth thoroughly. Then fold and roll the dry portion around the damp part until the entire cloth is uniformly damp.

To dampen a drill press cloth rub a wet sponge over the drill cloth to dampen it. A damp press cloth can also be used with a dry iron at higher temperatures when direct steam is required but the hot metal soleplate would harm the fabric. It also can be used for extra steam with a steam iron when your fabric requires more.

To minimize moisture, a dry press cloth can be used between fabric and steaming iron.

For added steam on water-sensitive fabrics, place a layer of drill cloth over the fabric. Then place a dampened cheesecloth over the drill cloth, or rub the back of it with a damp sponge.

Where much extra moisture is required on a small area—a buttonhole, for example—water can be applied directly with a small brush. Buy a toothbrush or pastry brush expressly for this purpose.

Be sure that the pressed area has dried and cooled slightly before moving it. Wool is best left slightly damp to dry naturally on the pressing board.

PRESSURE

The amount of pressure needed for successful construction pressing varies greatly with fiber and fabric. Some fabrics require the extra pressure of pounding with the wooden pounding block; on others steam from the iron may be enough to flatten construction details. Test your fabric carefully; if a fabric needs little pressure, its texture may be damaged by heavier pressure. Keep the weight of the iron in your hand so that you are pressing with less than the weight of the iron and pressure on the fabric is light. Be very careful to use a lifting and placing motion.

When extra pressure is needed, the pounding block is used to pound steam into the fabric. The iron is placed on the fabric over a press cloth to steam an area the length of the block; then iron and press cloth are removed, and the block is pounded on the area. This technique is usually reserved for very heavy fabrics or for a firmly tailored finish, but it may also be used to flatten seams, pleats, and facing edges in resilient fabrics. It is used extensively with wools because they are resilient and prone to shine.

1 steam iron
2 needleboard
3 white vinegar, brush, sponge
4 metal point
5 knitting needle
6 press mitt
7 pounding block
8 iron cover
9 pressing table, wool-backed drill cloth
10 edge and point presser
11 tailor's ham
12 cheesecloth
13 seam roll
14 sleeveboard

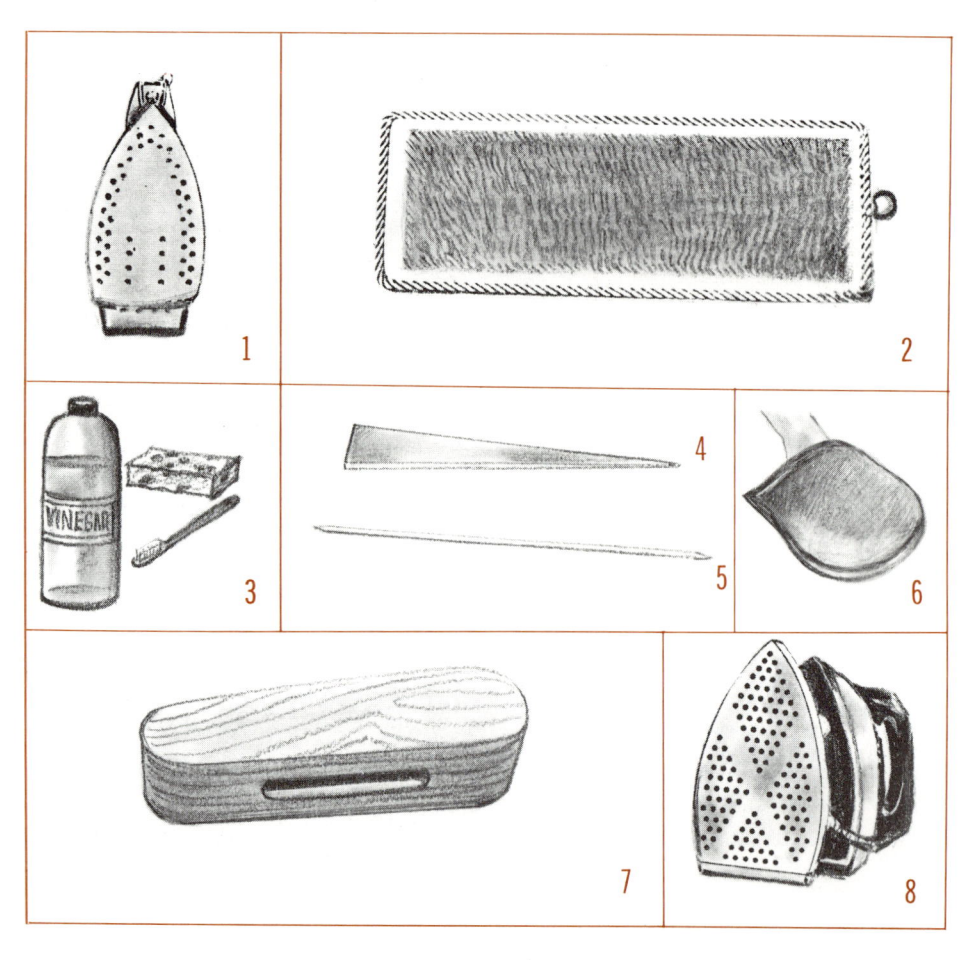

9

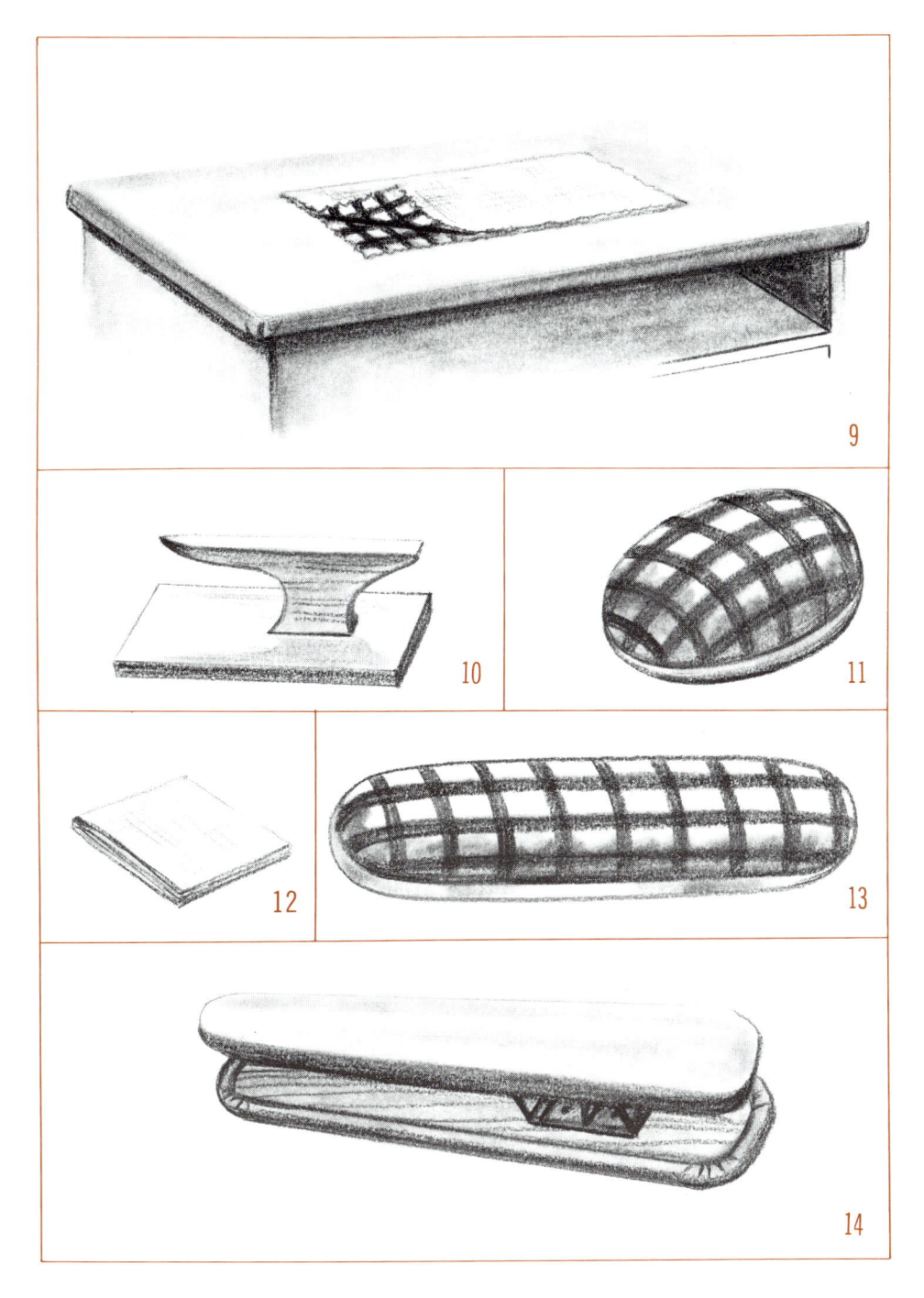

10

11

12

13

14

113

If a fabric looks overpressed even when touched lightly with the iron, try steaming it with the iron held above the surface. Light pressure may then be applied by placing, not pounding, the block on the area. Use a press mitt instead of a pounding block for an even softer finish.

For a very soft finish, steam your press mitt, and pat it lightly on the garment. Do not put the press mitt on your hand. You might use this method to press a soft, molded hem.

PROBLEMS IN PRESSING

There are three major problems in pressing. All can be prevented if you test-press your fabric carefully.

Iron shine may occur when a hot iron is placed in direct contact with a fabric. To prevent shine, always use a press cloth, and press from the wrong side whenever possible. For top pressing, heavy brown paper will also protect the fabric.

When iron shine develops it is hard to remove, but the following method may work. Wet a clean toothbrush slightly, and brush the shiny area either directly or through a drill cloth. Apply steam carefully, holding the iron about an inch above the fabric. Repeat this until the shine is gone. Some fabrics need to be brushed after they are steamed.

Waterspotting occurs on silks and other fabrics that are sensitive to moisture. Even steam from the iron may spot them. To prevent this, a piece of tissue paper or a thin press cloth should be used between iron and fabric. In extreme cases, a layer or two of drill cloth will be needed to control the moisture.

Unsightly impressions may form on the right side of fabric when construction details are pressed from the underside. To prevent this, insert strips of brown paper, paper toweling, or pieces of thin cardboard under seam allowances, darts, pleats, and buttonholes before pressing. Seams can also be prevented from leaving marks if they are pressed open over a seam roll or on the edge presser, with the point of the iron. If marks do occur, re-press under seam allowances, darts, and so on with point of iron.

FABRIC KNOWLEDGE

Your choice of heat, moisture, and pressing techniques will depend on the fiber content of your fabric and its construction. The care label you receive when you buy fabric has instructions for care of fabric. The heat-setting guide on your iron lists the specific heat setting on that iron recommended for each fiber type. The newest irons list brand names under each fiber type so that you can recognize your fabric easily. Both care label and heat-setting guide will be helpful in the overall care of your finished garment.

Using all the information you have, try the recommendations on fabric scraps before doing construction to determine exactly how your fabric should be pressed. Following are additional factors to consider for some fabrics frequently used for tailoring.

Wool should be carefully steam-pressed. Too much moisture may cause shrinkage. A lack of it will cause the wool to become brittle. Leave wool slightly damp from the steam to dry on the ironing board. Self-fabric makes a good press cloth, especially for napped woolens. Smooth fabrics like gabardine will need a layer of drill cloth to protect them from the steam.

Polyester is pressed with steam and medium heat. Press from the wrong side to avoid shine. A heavy polyester knit may have to be steam-pressed on the right side; be sure to use a press cloth.

Silk fibers are weakened by too much heat. Press from the wrong side with steam at medium heat. Tissue or a thin press cloth next to the fabric will prevent waterspotting. When pressing satin, use one or two layers of drill between steam iron and fabric. Some silks will press well without moisture.

Knits should be handled carefully during construction pressing so they will not stretch out of shape. Do not let garment pieces hang over the edge of your ironing board unless they are supported by a stool or countertop of the same height. Press lightly on the lengthwise grain on the wrong side of the fabric. If you must press on the right side,'protect the fabric with a press cloth. If your test-pressing reveals a tendency to shine, try steaming the seams with the iron held above the fabric and then finger-pressing. Heavy knits need strips of paper toweling or brown paper under darts and seam allowances to prevent ridges on the right side.

Napped fabrics should be pressed face down on a piece of self-fabric or Turkish toweling. This surface will help keep the nap from matting. The fabric will look fresher if the nap is brushed lightly with a clothes brush while it is still slightly damp.

Pile fabrics vary a great deal. The pile may be very short, or it may be deep and furry. It is important to use pressing methods that will not harm the texture of the fabric. The short-pile fabrics, corduroy and velveteen, can be pressed successfully if they are placed face down on a piece of self-fabric or Turkish toweling. Press lightly and, as much as possible, from the wrong side. Use a needleboard for pressing velvet.

EQUIPMENT

The equipment and accessories needed to successfully tailor a garment are shown on pages 112–113.

Press boards and sleeve boards should be very well padded for tailoring. The press board can be built as a table with shelves below, or it can be built for use on top of a table. Garment fabric rests on table surface while it is being pressed, preventing fabric from stretching, which can occur on an ironing board. Attach short legs to raise board to a comfortable height for pressing. Pad both pressing and sleeve board as follows:

Use enough layers of wool (an old blanket would be excellent) to make padding ⅜ to ½ inch (1 to 1.3cm) thick. For a sleeve board you will probably want to draw a paper pattern of the board. Stagger the size of the layers. Make each ½ inch (1.3cm) smaller all around the one beneath. Tack layers together by hand to keep them from slipping.

Fasten the padding to the board with largest layer on top. Padding can be nailed to wood, of course. Use glue to fasten edges of padding to a metal sleeve board. Make a removable cover from unbleached muslin. Cut cover on the bias. Stitch elastic to edge of cover so that it will fit board snugly.

A pressing cushion or tailor's ham is a ham-shaped pillow, firmly packed with wool scraps. Areas of a garment that should be curved are pressed over the ham to give them shaping. Hams of various sizes are commercially available, but you can make one yourself. Stitch two ovals of fabric together, leaving an open end. Turn to the right side and stuff tightly with wool scraps. Close the open end with hand stitching. The most useful cushion will have one side covered with drill or firm muslin and the other with wool.

A press mitt is a small curved cushion with a pocket to slip over your hand. It is also used to shape curved areas of the garment. Sometimes the commercial ones are not stuffed full enough to provide the needed shaping, but you can rip a seam, stuff in some wool, and sew it up again.

A seam or sleeve roll is used to press small curved areas of a garment as well as the seams in sleeves and pant legs. It is made in the same way as the ham.

An edge and point presser is made of wood. The many edges and small flat surfaces are used for pressing hard-to-reach seams, cuffs, and collar points.

The wooden clapper or pounding block forces steam into the fabric and flattens it so that you can obtain sharp edges on heavy and resilient fabrics. It is used when you want crisp tailored edges, as in pleats and seams, but you can achieve a softer effect by merely placing the block on top of the steamed fabric.

ACCESSORIES AND PRESS CLOTHS

An attachment that fits over the soleplate of your iron is designed to permit steam from the iron to penetrate fabric but prevents the hot metal of the soleplate from scorching or causing shine.

The use of filtered or distilled water will help you keep your steam iron in good condition. The minerals in natural water can accumulate to clog the steam holes. There is a variety of home filtering equipment, or you can buy distilled water by the bottle.

A needleboard prevents pile fabrics from matting. The board is made of very fine wires embedded in canvas. When the fabric is placed face down on the board and steamed from the wrong side, the wires separate the pile and keep it from flattening.

Cheesecloth will provide the extra moisture that is sometimes needed even when you are steampressing. A yard in grade 70 is a good buy. Many fabrics—cottons, for example—press professionally with dampened cheesecloth directly on them.

There are some commercial press cloths that are chemically treated to insure that only steam, not water, penetrates them.

Drill cloth is used to protect fabric that cannot take moisture directly. Wash to remove any starch before using.

A drill cloth faced with wool helps to prevent flattening a textured woolen. They are available commercially but you can make one yourself. Sew a piece of wool to drill cloth, and pink the edges.

A piece of self-fabric is useful for pressing a napped or short-pile fabric. Use the right side of the piece face down on right side of garment. A remnant of mohair upholstery also makes a successful and durable press cloth for nap fabrics.

A sponge should be handy to moisten the drill cloth as necessary and to mop up spills.

White vinegar is excellent for removing shine and creases in fabric—for example, hemlines that have been let down. The vinegar can be painted on these areas with a narrow paint brush. Steam press after it has been applied.

Use a metal knitting needle or a piece of metal cut to a point to divide darts in heavy fabric for pressing.

An old toothbrush or a small paint brush can be used to brush extra moisture onto a specific area, either on the drill cloth or directly on the garment (to press a buttonhole, for example).

CONSTRUCTION PRESSING

It is essential to a professional product to press as you sew. Keep the iron heated and your pressing boards near your machine as you make your garment. A rule to remember is never to cross a seam or dart with another seam until it has been permanent-stitched, the basting has been removed, and it has been pressed.

SEAMS

Sequences for pressing can be found under the specific construction. Most plain seams are pressed open, except in the following cases:

1. A seam is not pressed open when a detail requires that it lie in a certain direction (as for topstitching).
2. At the back of a pleat, seam allowances stay together.
3. A waistline seam is pressed up toward the bodice.
4. Any seam that joins a gathered edge to a plain edge is pressed with both seam allowances turned toward the plain side.
5. From one notch to the other in the underarm area, the armhole seam is not pressed at all. From one notch to the other over the top, the seam allowances lie together into the sleeve, but are not pressed flat. Press with the point of the iron at the seamline, using a ham or the edge of a sleeve board.

Before you press a seam open, press it flat along the line of stitching. This will help the stitches sink into the fabric and give a smoother look to the seamline.

Then pull the seam apart by placing your hands to the right and left of the seam and smoothing the fabric away from the line of stitching. Open the seam with your fingers, and using a dry iron, press along the line of stitching with the point of your iron. Apply moisture (if appropriate for the fabric), and press the seam flat.

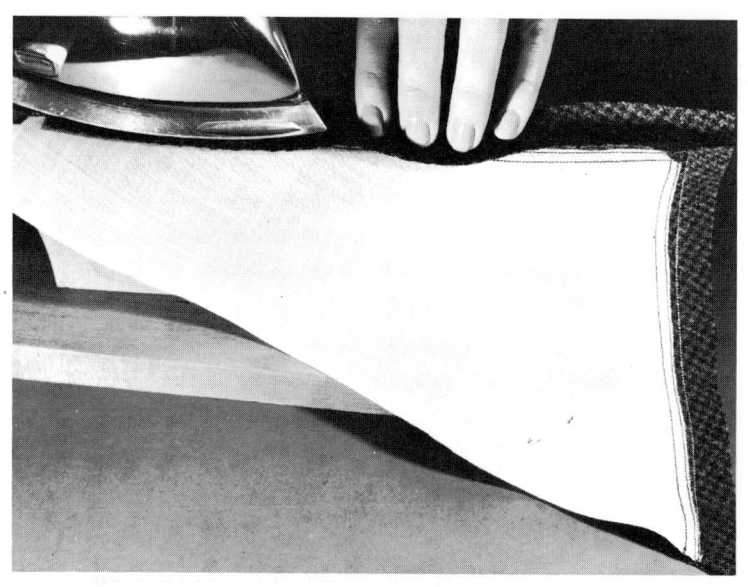

The edge and point presser is used to press open seams on collars and facings before they are trimmed, turned, and closed. When they are pressed on the outside, the edges will lie smoothly and flat without a well or groove at the stitching line.

BLOCKING

A garment is given contour with darts, curved seams, seams with ease, and similar construction details, by pressing, and by blocking.

Areas to be blocked on the cushion are carefully placed over it on grain on a section of the cushion where they fit properly. The following parts of a garment are never pressed flat on a pressing board, but are molded or blocked to the figure on a cushion:
1. Side seams above hip notches on a straight skirt.
2. Waistline seams. (If the waistline is too small or does not fit the cushion because of the style, it is better to press this seam on an edge presser.)
3. As a rule, all darts except those in a skirt front should be pressed on a cushion to shape the garment properly.
4. The shoulders of a garment must be shaped to fit the body.
5. Any zipper in a curved garment seam should be pressed on a cushion.

When you are ready to press, take time to place your garment carefully on the board or cushion. Be sure it is placed so that you can press it on grain. It may take longer to press a part of the garment than it did to stitch it, but this will make more sense to you as you begin to see how vital careful construction pressing is to the finished garment. Each seam, dart, and detail must be pressed and shaped in the proper direction.

To block a shoulder, place shoulder seam wrong side up over curve of cushion, just as it will lie over the shoulder. Press seam open from neckline to armhole. Then turn garment to right side and mold back shoulderline by pressing on lengthwise grain along edge of cushion so the garment will fit the curve of the back shoulder. A diagonal sleeve seam on a cut-on sleeve should be held firmly on the lengthwise grain as it is being pressed open.

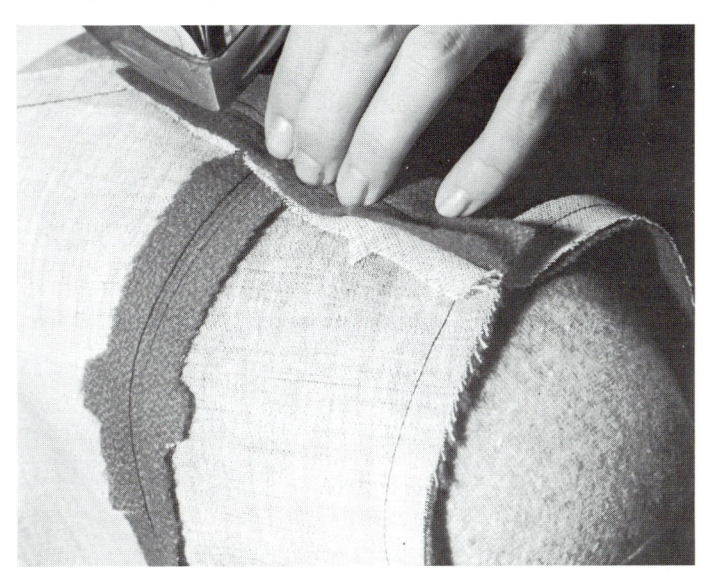

A zipper placed in any curved seam of a garment should be pressed over a cushion to shape the area to the curve of the body. Close zipper. Whenever possible, press from the wrong side. No matter what side you are pressing, use a press cloth, and place strips of paper or cardboard under the placket lap, if there is one. Do not press directly on the zipper teeth.

POUNDING BLOCK

After edges have been set in place with the iron, the pounding block is used on the outside of the garment to obtain sharp, thin edges without iron shine on wool and other heavy fabrics. Steam an area the exact length of the block, quickly remove iron (and steam-iron cloth or drill cloth and cheesecloth, if used), and slap garment with the block. This forces out the steam and leaves flat, sharp edges. Repeat if necessary. The pounding block is used mainly in tailoring on buttonholes, lapels, collars, facings, hems, pleats, pockets. It is never used on the zipper. It is not used extensively in pressing when fashion requires a softer look at edges.

If fabric has pile or nap, a cloth mitt aids in flattening these areas. Certain pile or nap fabrics may be pounded with a piece of their own fabric on top, right side down. It is placed before applying steam and is not removed until the pounding is completed.

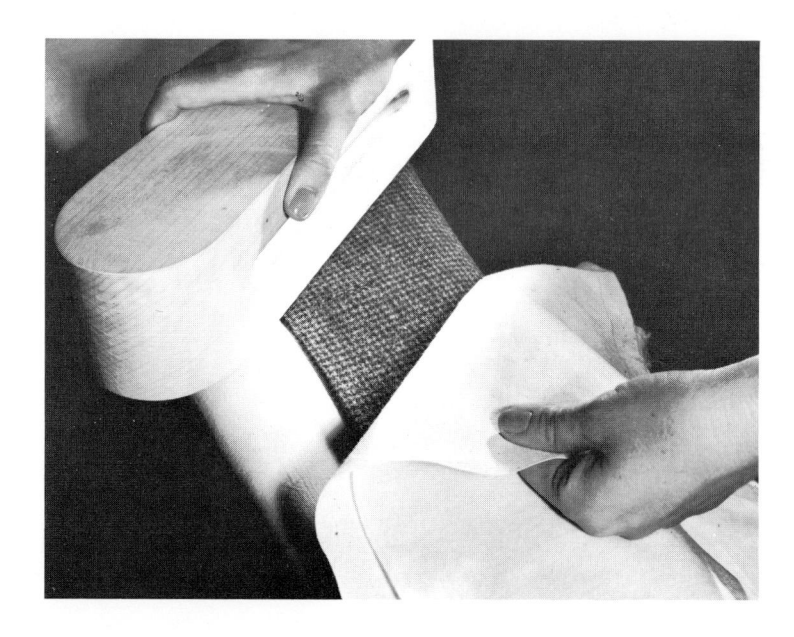

FINAL PRESSING

The final pressing and the attention given to the garment at this time complete the change from fabric to flawless garment. This should be done before lining is inserted. The amount of work necessary will depend on the quality of your construction pressing and on the characteristics of your fabric.

Remove any baste stitching that remains. Brush lint and stray threads from the garment. Examine the fabric for iron shine, iron marks, wrinkles, and areas that need special attention.

Press a garment in the following sequence: collar, sleeves, shoulders, facings, bodice front, bodice back, and skirt.

Holding the steam iron ½ to 1 inch (1.3-2.5cm) away, allow steam to penetrate fabric to remove shine, to raise nap, and to remove an overpressed look.

Touch up all key points—neck and armhole edges, facings, zipper, and hem. Always follow correct grain directions. If necessary, go over darts and seams again from the wrong side. Press lightly to prevent edges from leaving an impression on the outside of the garment or use cardboard strips under seam allowances and construction details.

Use the cushion and pounding block wherever they were used in construction pressing. If details on a deep-pile fabric must be pressed again, use the needle board. Use the specific techniques given in the fabric section for the fabrics mentioned there.

The final pressing is done on the right side of the garment unless the fabric absolutely prevents this, as in the case of velvet. Be sure to use an appropriate press cloth. Brown paper or tissue paper (if the iron is not too hot) make good press cloths here, as they leave no troublesome lint on your fabric.

A collar and lapel should be molded and shaped over a cushion as one unit. Use the iron carefully on the lengthwise grain (see photo, page 41).

Sleeves should not be creased. Press them over a seam roll. Always press hem with the lengthwise grain. Press lightly and carefully. Move the iron up and down, never across. Place a narrow skirt over the edge of the press board. A garment with a full skirt can be pressed to greater perfection if the hem is laid out the length of the press board. Remove basting from pleats. Do not press over the line where hem was stitched to garment, or it will be emphasized. A soft hem may be steamed and patted lightly with a press mitt rather than pressed. Dry hem thoroughly before moving garment.

The zipper area should be touched up carefully. Follow the techniques suggested for construction pressing, page 122. Keep zipper closed while pressing.

When you are satisfied with the details of your garment, hang it on a dress form or padded hanger. If you wish, you can fill out the neckline and shoulders with tissue. Then, holding the iron about 3 inches (7.5cm) away from fabric, steam garment, patting and molding it into shape with your hands. Do not use your hands or any iron pressure on the right side of a deep-pile fabric; for final steaming, hang the garment on a padded hanger in a steam-filled bathroom. Let the garment dry before touching it.

INDEX

armholes
   in linings, 46, 54–56
   pressing, 119

belts, 62
beveling, 37, 109
bias, 14, 17–18, 42
blocking, 42, 120–122
bulk, handling of
   in belts and waistbands, 62
   in coat facings, 92
   in corners, 24
   in pockets, 108
   in seamlines, 33
bust darts, 23
buttonholes, 63, 86–89
buttons, 83–85

chalk and pins for marking, 20
changing points to curves, 90
checks, plaids, stripes, 12
cheesecloth, 110, 111, 112, 118
closures, 82–89
coats, 41
   interlining, 90–93
   lining, 52, 92–93
   See also facings, garment back, garment front, sleeves.
collars, 33–40
   bias, 14, 37
   changing points to curves in, 90
   cutting, 14
   extra notches, 13
   fusible interfacings in, 61–62
   in heavy fabrics, 14
   interfacings in, 14
   pressing, 35–36, 40–41, 123
   roll lines, 34, 61–62
corduroy, 6, 116
curved seams, 72
curves from points, 90
cut-on sleeves, 56, 71, 121
cutting
   collar, 14–15
   garment fabric, 11–14
   interfacing, 15–18
   lining, 44–46

darts, 22–23
   blocking, 120
   in fusible interfacings, 59, 61
   in interfacings, 23
   in interlinings, 91
   marking, 17, 19, 20
   pressing, 23, 123
direction of nap, 11–12
drill cloths, 111, 112, 118

ease
   in front facings, 31
   in hems, 41
   in linings, 45, 48, 52
   in pockets, 108
   in sleevecaps, 28–29, 56

edge and point pressers, 40, 117, 120
extra notches on patterns, 13

fabrics
  choosing, 5–7
  for interlinings, 90–91
  piecing, 72–73
  preparing, 10
  pressing requirements, 115–116
  storing, 10
  See also corduroy, heavy fabrics, knits, lightweight fabrics, medium-weight fabrics, napped fabrics, non-wool fabrics, velveteen, water-sensitive fabrics, wool.
facings, 60, 66–71, 90
  sewing, 30–33
  foldback, 60, 66–67
  holding in position, 90
  interfacings with, 15–16, 17, 66–67
finishing strips for buttonholes, 87–88
flap (tab) pockets, 107–109
flaps (tabs) without pockets, 94–95
foldback facings, 60, 66–71
four-point closures (collar and lapel), 40
fusible interfacings, 57–63

garment back
  fusible interfacings, 60–61
  interfacings for, 17, 24–26
  joining to front, 26
  staystitching, 26
garment front, 26, 58–60
  construction, 22–24
  interfacing for, 58–60, 63, 71
grading seams, 32, 37, 40, 44
grainlines, 14, 110
grosgrain for waistbands, 82

hand picking, 78
heavy or bulky fabrics, 33
  beveling, 37
  collars in, 14
  facings in, 30
  pattern reinforcement for, 13
  waistbands in, 80
  welt pockets for, 100–103
hems, 41–44, 62, 93
  bias strips for, 17–18, 62
  fusible interfacing in, 62
  pressing, 42, 62, 123–124
  staystitch plus, 62
  take-up tucks in, 52–53

interfacing
  capes and cut-on sleeves, 71
  collars, 14, 34, 60–61, 66–69
  flaps (tabs), 107
  front facings, 15–16, 60, 66–67
  garment backs, 17, 24–26, 60–61, 71
  garment fronts, 58–60, 69, 71
  hems, 17–18, 29, 62
  knit jackets, unlined, 59
  to lift shoulders, 26, 65
  pockets, 107
  with underlining, 69–71
  waistbands, 80
interfacings
  applying fusible, 58–62
  choosing, 7–8
  cutting, 13–16, 58, 59, 66
  darts in, 23
  fusible, 57–63
  grain of, 8, 15, 16
  handling at corners, 24
  lightweight, 17
  non-woven, 7–8
  piecing, 72–73

staystitching, 24
   with underlining, 69–71
   woven, 7, 8, 10
interlinings, 90–93

jackets, 22–44, 60–61, 78
   See also linings.

knits
   tailoring, 57–63
   pressing, 115–116

labels, 79
lapels
   corners in, 24
   fusible interfacings, 59
   interfacings, 24
   pressing, 40, 123
   in relation to buttonholes, 11
   roll line reinforcement in, 59
   topstitching, 75, 77
layout, 11–12, 14–15
lightweight fabrics
   interfacing, 66
   modified welt pockets for, 104–106
   as under collars in bulky fabrics, 14
linings, 44–57
   choosing fabric, 5–6, 8–9
   for coats, 52, 92–93
   cutting, 44–46
   garment, sewing, 47–48
   garment, inserting, 50–56
   pocket, 96–97
   preparing, 10
   pressing, 48, 56
   sleeve, inserting, 49–50

marking, 18–21

napped fabrics
   laying out and cutting, 11–12
   preparing, 10
   pressing, 116, 122
non-wool fabrics, tailoring, 57–63
needleboards, 112, 117–118

off-grain stitching for sleeve caps, 27
one-way designs, 12

patch pockets, 96–99
patterns
   adding notches, 13
   choosing, 5–6
   modifying, 11
pickup lines, 19
pile fabrics
   laying out and cutting, 11
   pressing, 116, 122, 123
pleats, 78, 119
pockets
   fantastic patch, 96–99
   flap (tab), 107–109
   flap (tab) only, 94–95
   interfacing of, 62, 107
   modified welt, 103–106
   welt, 100–103
polyester, 6, 8, 115
pounding block, 32, 74, 108, 111, 112, 117, 122, 123
press board, 116
press cloths, 117–118
press cushion, 40, 117, 123
press mitt, 114, 117
pressing, 22–23, 44, 118–124
   accessories, 117–118
   construction, 118–120
   equipment, 112–113, 116–117
   final, 123–124

pressing (continued)
  fusibles, 62
  garment before lining, 44
  pressure in, 111, 114
  problems, 114
  moisture in, 110–111
  specific fabrics, 115–116
  to straighten grain, 10
  water-sensitive fabrics, 111
  See also blocking and construction details (collars, darts, seams, etc.).

reinforcement
  of buttons, 84–85
  of collar roll lines, 61–62
  of facing edge, 66
  of lapel roll lines, 59
  of pockets, 99, 104, 107
  stitching of lapels, 31

seam roll, 29, 112–113, 117
seams
  bulky, 33
  grading, 32, 37, 40, 44
  pressing, 119–120
set-in sleeves, 27–30, 48–50
shoulder shapes, 64
shoulders
  blocking, 120–121
  extra interfacing at, 61, 65
  shapes for, 64
sleeve headings, 73
sleeveboards, 116
sleevecaps, 13, 27–28, 56
sleeves, 17
  cut-on, 56, 71, 121
  headings for, 73
  hemming, 28
  interlining, 91

inserting in garment, 30
  lining, 45–50
  pleat openings, 78
  pressing, 29, 117, 123
  set-in, 27–30
snaps, 82–83
staystitch plus, 34, 41–42, 62
staystitching
  facings, 30
  garment back, 24, 26
  garment front, 24
  interlinings, 92
  linings, 47
  waistbands, 81

tailor's ham, 117
tailor's tacks, 20–21
take-up tucks, 49, 52–53
thread tracing, 19
topstitching, 34, 73–77
tracing paper and wheel, 18–19
trial garments, 10–11
turn-of-the-cloth, 33, 68–70, 95, 97

underlinings, 8, 68–72

velveteen, 6, 116, 123

waistbands, 13, 62, 80–82
waistline darts, 23
waistline seams, 119–120
waterspotting, 114
welt pockets, 100–106
wool, 6, 10, 115

zippers, 80, 120, 122, 124

128